CHAPEL
IN MY
HEART

BRIGITTE MACKO

Chapel In My Heart
Copyright © 2021 by Brigitte Macko

All rights reserved. No part of this publication may be reproduced, distributed, or transmitted in any form or by any means, including photocopying, recording, or other electronic or mechanical methods, without the prior written permission of the publisher or author, except in the case of brief quotations embodied in critical reviews and certain other noncommercial uses permitted by copyright law.

Although every precaution has been taken to verify the accuracy of the information contained herein, the author and publisher assume no responsibility for any errors or omissions. No liability is assumed for damages that may result from the use of information contained within.

Library of Congress Control Number: 2021902592
ISBN-13:   Paperback: 978-1-64749-362-2
            ePub: 978-1-64749-363-9

Printed in the United States of America

GoToPublish LLC
1-888-337-1724
www.gotopublish.com
info@gotopublish.com

Chapel In My Heart

Brigitte Macko

Table of Contents

The First Miracle 1
The Angel Whisper 2
The Escape! 4
Another Miracle 6
Miracle Four 7
God Has a Sense of Humor, Ya Think? 9
Li'l Escape Artist! 11
Mother Knows Best! 13
Where Is the Good Doctor When You Need Him? 15
Little Chicken 17
Second Miracle for My "Miracle Baby" 18
Failed Suicide 20
The Fifth Miracle 22
Is There a Lifeguard on Duty? 23
The Little Wanderer/Wanderlust 27
James Street Miracle 30
Blood Poisoning 32
Will the Owner Please Call the Police? 36
The Second Husband 37
Sometimes You See It Coming, Sometimes You Don't! 40
What Is a Hurricane? 42
Chapter 1979 49
Husband #3 54
Another Divine Intervention 60
Fireworks of a Different Kind 61

Demolition Derby	63
Mopsy Dies and Saves Lives!	66
Larry's Nose	68
I Think God Plays Chess	70
Workman's Compensation	72
The First Eleventh Hour	78
The Vision	81
Camping Trailer Went A-WOL	82
Interlude	84
Please Don't Cremate My Steak! (I Like It Medium-Rare)	85
Paranormal Activity 2004	88
Paranormal Activity Abe Lincoln	90
Angel Vision	93
The Second Eleventh Hour	99
Angel Whispers in My Front Yard	104
Evil Lurks Close By	107
Secret Wishes, Instant Answers!	109
Highway to Heaven	111
Dove or Pigeon?	114
Channel Surfing	115
High-Flying Books	117
Visit from the Evil One	119
Abe Lincoln Is Still Here	121
Prayer Booth	122
Worms	123
Revelation 1	124
Present Times	126
Second and Third Revelation	127
Good Friday	129
Rosary	131
God Knows What You Need	133
God Doesn't Lie, He Keeps His Promises!	135
Gruesome Vision	137
The Third Wrath	138
Last Page of Book	140
Faith, Believe, Love	143

This book is dedicated to my four daughters:

>Patricia,
>Carla
>Heidi and Jennifer

My four grandchildren:

>Destiny
>Reef
>Jonathan and
>Andrew

Special mention to my daughter Carla, who diligently deciphered my handwriting and typed the whole book. Carla, you will get your reward in Heaven. Smile

May God bless you with good health and a long happy life.

Love Mom
Liebe mutti

Prologue

September 2017

If anyone had told me as little as six months ago that I would be writing this "booklet," I would have said, "No way, not I." This idea would have been so outlandish and farfetched. When I first came to this country in 1966, I developed an inferiority complex. Every time I opened my mouth, someone would ask me "Where are you from? Do I detect an accent?" I wanted to be like everyone else. I felt I didn't speak English well enough, and my vocabulary was limited. I spoke Oxford English with a heavy German accent. No one could understand what I was saying. It was embarrassing and frustrating. I might as well have had spoken Chinese. At that time, I always carried paper and pencil with me so I could write down what I was trying to say. Finally, I met a neighbor who was from Pennsylvania. She grew up near an Amish settlement and understood my accent. She interpreted my English so the other neighbors knew what I was saying.

When my oldest daughter Patricia was only two and a half years old, she said, "Mommy, you talk funny." Out of the mouths of babes!

At one time, I took a course at Syracuse University. It was called "Native Tongue." I was elated. Now, finally, I would learn how to speak like everyone else. I wouldn't be a foreigner any longer. Wow! Yeah, twelve weeks and $900 later, I could perfectly speak and write—I haffta, I gotta, I wanna. I got an A. Not exactly what I had in mind. No one detected an accent there. (Smile.)

When my youngest daughter Jennifer was around thirteen years old, I answered the phone one day to a young man calling and asking to speak with her. I told him she wasn't home, and I asked him if he would like to leave a message. He said, "No I'll see her in class tomorrow." The next day he said to Jennifer, "Your mom must be rich!" My daughter asked him whatever made him assume this. His reply was "I called your house yesterday and your Spanish maid answered the phone." Smile.

The First Miracle

I was born on March 12, 1944 in Schwabisch Gmund, Germany. In June 1944, the sirens for an air-raid went off all over town. Everyone ran down to the basement. My grandmother, mother, and her sister met in the basement. That is when they realized I was missing. My mother had my four-year old sister but forgot about me. She refused to go back up. I was on the third floor, in a glass-enclosed veranda. The bombing started. The Americans bombed the railroad tracks one and a half miles away from our house so Hitler could not send any more troops, food, medical supplies, guns, ammunition, etc. to the front lines. My aunt rushed up to get me. Every window was broken, broken glass was everywhere, even in my bassinet, and I was unharmed. If any one of the glass pieces had embedded itself in my little body, I would have died. No buildings or lives were lost. As told by my grandmother.

The Angel Whisper

When I was five, my mother took me to see my father's parents in Oberndorf, near Rudersberg. We could only visit every two to three years. My father's parents had thirteen children—three girls first and then ten boys. The youngest, number twelve and thirteen were twins. One of the twins died in a fire at the age of two. He played with matches and his clothes caught on fire. My father was the other twin. There was also a half-brother. My grandfather was married before. The woman didn't want any more children, so he divorced her. He went to Switzerland on business, met my grandmother, and brought her to Germany.

So all ten boys were drafted into Hitler's army and stationed in different cities. All of them married women in those cities and had anywhere from three to four children. In Germany, we had only four weeks of summer vacation. So every year, for one week only, all of the daughters-in-law would visit with the grandchildren. That was only four families a year. We had to take turns. The only four cousins I had met were the ones who lived upstairs in my grandparents' home.

I was the youngest and no one paid much attention to me. They were all older, and who wanted to play with a "baby"? On one of their visits, I had it in my mind that I wanted to ride a bike. The girls were teenagers and had new bicycles—the old style, with heavy balloon tires. I went into the shed, pushed out a bike, and started to go on one. I was too short to reach the seat. At first, I wobbled all over the place and just rode around the courtyard. After a while, I realized that the faster I went, the steadier the ride. So I ventured out onto the road. It was in the country, with hardly any traffic, so I had clear sailing. I had no idea where I was or where I was going, I just peddled straight ahead faster and faster. It was exhilarating. All of a sudden, the road took a nosedive. I found myself going downhill, faster and faster. All of a sudden, a train appeared at the bottom of the hill around the bend. At first I thought, *Well, it'll be gone by the time I get there.* Halfway down, I became afraid because the train seemed endless. I looked to the right at the locomotive, followed it with my eyes to the left, and hoped that every car was the last one appearing around the bend. They were coming, coming, and coming! Freight cars were a lot longer than passenger cars. Now, I wanted to stop, but I didn't know how. There were no brakes on the handlebars. Now, I was scared stiff. I didn't know you had to put the pedals in reverse. I realized that I would hit the train head-on and I was paralyzed with fear; I thought I would die. Then I heard a voice in my head, *Jump off the bike!* I slightly turned my head, but there was no one. My first thought was that if there is a car behind me, I'll die too. I did nothing. Then I heard the voice again, more forceful this time, *Jump off the bike!* Without thinking this time, I jumped off to the left; no cars were behind me. I was no worse for the wear. I had only skinned knees. The handlebars were turned a little sideways. I had to push them back into place. No one was outside when I returned, so I put the bike back in the shed. When my uncle, Adolph, asked me what happened, I just said I climbed up a tree and fell off. I was a tomboy and liked to climb trees, so it was believable. No one ever mentioned the bike.

What astonishes me today is, that I was able to judge the distance and the speed. I'm sure something or someone put that in my head.

The Escape!

1949

Here is a miraculous story of escape as told to me as a young child. When I was four or five, all of a sudden, my uncle Cornelius came into my life. He was my father's oldest sister Marie's husband. He was also drafted into Hitler's army. This story was so incredible I asked him to tell me more just in case he forgot something. He had been captured by the Russians during World War II and had to work in the coal mines in Siberia. He escaped but was recaptured and sent back. He escaped a second time and wandered around in circles for three years. He had no idea the war was even over. I asked him a million questions.

Now, I grew up brushing my teeth three times a day, my hair was braided, not a single strand could come loose, my oma checked my fingernails, behind my ears, etc. before being sent to kindergarten. My shoes had to be polished every day, clothes ironed, no missing buttons on sweaters, no sleeping in clothes, etc. You get the picture.

Now, of course, I had to ask.

"Uncle, how did you brush your teeth?"

He replied, "Just with my finger."

"Uncle, how did you comb your hair?"

"I didn't" was his reply.

"Uncle, how did you take a bath?"

"Only in the summer in a river" was his reply.

"Where did you sleep?"

"I climbed up a tree and tied myself onto the highest branch I thought would support me so that the bears couldn't climb up as far as me."

"Well, what did you eat?"

"I ate mushrooms berries, tree bark, etc., and I caught fish in the river."

"Where did you get a fishing pole, bait-line, etc.?"

He said, "I caught them with my bare hands."

"How did you cook it?"

"I didn't. I was afraid to make a fire and give away my location."

"How did you wash and iron your clothes?

"I didn't, I stole clean clothes off clotheslines from farmers. Sometimes I got caught and was run off the property by a farmer. Sometimes they gave me food. Sometimes I would wait until nighttime and sleep in a barn under the haystack."

One time, he said he woke up with a pitchfork around his neck. The man let him go, realizing he meant no harm. He had a feeling that the man had no idea there even was a war going on. My uncle also said that, in the winter, when it was freezing, he never took off his boots. The reason why is that while he was still with his unit marching toward Moscow, some of his comrades took off their boots. Their legs were so frozen that their feet would snap off completely. Their blood was also frozen. They had to leave their comrades behind. After three years, he finally reached Austria, a German-speaking country, where he realized that the war had been over for three years. He got home via hopping freight trains.

To my child's mind, that was truly miraculous and still is! His brother-in-law, my father's half-brother Julius, had three little girls. His wife died in childbirth with number three. Cornelius and my father's sister, Marie, took the three little girls into their home and raised them as their own. They were not blessed with children themselves. I'd like to think this was the reason God saved his life.

Another Miracle

1950

When I was six, I lived with my grandmother—my mother's mother—and I asked my grandmother if I could have skis. So I went to a hill where other kids were tobogganing and skiing. I watched them and did what they did, snow-plowed to stop, take turns, go up sideways in small steps, etc. The shop where my oma bought all my ski clothes and equipment had a contest, a race. So of course I went. At the bottom, every participant was awarded with a hotdog. I came in third in my age group. Hmm, not bad for teaching myself. Well, I went back up the hill, thinking that if I go back down, I'd get another hotdog. By the time I was back on top, I was tired and cold. I wanted to go home. So I figured I'd ski down the hill via the streets. It didn't have a lot of turns, skiing around trees, potholes, etc. The roads were hard and icy. There's only one—what we called hairpin curve. As I got closer, I realized that if I made a sharp turn, I would hydroplane into the other lane and possibly have a head-on collision with a car. You couldn't see what was coming. Well, I didn't hear a voice, but a calm came over me, and I just decided to "go with the flow." Then I also saw another problem. There was a stairway on the other side that led to another crossroad. The railing was a long skinny log. Now I was visualizing myself hitting the railing with my stomach and the railing protruding out of my back. I had prayed every night for my guardian angel to keep me safe. That gave me peace of mind. Miraculously, I flew across the road, no cars coming, missed the railing, and my skis went hobble, hobble, hobble down the steps and into the crossroad; no car in sight there either. The incline dropped, and I was able to stop, take a deep breath, and ski on home. I never said a word to anyone. I was afraid my oma would take my skis away—"for my own good," of course.

Miracle Four

1951

When I was seven, my mother's cousin, Fritz (Friedrich), got married. I called him Uncle Fritz and his wife, Tante Gerda. They had a little boy. I was allowed to push him around the block in his baby carriage. When he was two years old and I was nine, Tante Gerda asked me to come and take little Fritzle sledding. Behind the garage was a hill where all the neighbors' kids went sledding and skiing. At the bottom was a pond, frozen over. The older children had hacked a hole in the ice and skied over it. The challenge was to ski over the whole without falling in and not tipping the skis into it but gliding over it. Little Fritz got excited and shouted, "Me too, me too!"

I held him tightly, and of course, I said "No, No." I had padded ski mittens on and he did too. He had wriggled his little hand out of his mitten and ran. He ran toward that hole. I was holding his mitten in mine. I hadn't felt it and took off immediately to catch him, but I wasn't fast enough. Instead of jumping over the hole, he jumped right into it. Without thinking about my safety, I jumped in right after him. All I could think of was *Save Fritz from drowning!* I was able to grab his coat, pull him up to where the older kids pulled him out onto the ice, and then helped me. So we walked back to the house. The door was locked. No one was home. Tante Gerda went to town to shop. So we sat on the porch steps soaking wet, shivering, wearing clothing turned to ice. We sat there at least two hours. I thought we would freeze to death. Tante Gerda finally came home, gave little Fritzle a warm bath, and sent me home two miles, where my Oma did the same. Later on, I was astonished to realize that not only one, but three or four miracles had occurred: (1) Fritzle sat still on the bottom of the pond, he didn't wiggle around or panic, and he didn't swallow water; (2) I was able to find him right away. I couldn't see anything, I just felt around for him; (3) I found the "opening" to come up; and (4) we could've caught pneumonia later on while waiting or died of hypothermia. Two little lives could have tragically ended. Our guardian angels were at work. There was no time for whispers, only action. Every night, I ended my prayers, "Dear guardian angels, please keep me safe." Now, seventy-three-plus years later, I realize just how busy I kept mine!

God Has a Sense of Humor, Ya Think?

1958

I was raised by my oma. All of a sudden, when I was fourteen, my mother took a little interest in me. I found it odd. Sometimes, on Sunday noon around 4:00 PM, tea time, she asked me to accompany her to visit some of her friends. They were mostly widowed like herself. Soon, I realized they all had something in common. All were well off and all had at least one son between eighteen and twenty-two years of age. She had bought me my first pair of high heels and nylon stockings. Really, Mom? What was she thinking? I was a tomboy, played soccer, and climbed trees! The pantyhose hadn't been invented back then, 1958, so I had to wear a garter belt and hook them up. I hated that thing. The stockings also had seams in the back. They had to be straight as a rod. Her tailor showed up and took my measurements. I had to choose the style and the fabric. Mostly straight dresses with matching jackets or coats, and wool for winter, silk for summer. I always felt uncomfortable. "*M*e, play 'lady?'" and I had to sit straight up on their sofas, legs straight, closed not crossed. Heaven forbid someone see a little leg past my knees. I had to hold the saucer in my left hand, elbow close to my side, and a teacup in my right hand and do the little pinky thing, arm close to my side, bringing the cup up to my lips and take little sips. Etiquette dictated that you sat with the straight back and brought the cup to your lips. You could not bend your upper body or head down to meet the cup. That would have been an unforgivable gesture and made you an outcast or unsuitable prospects for their sons!

There was a lady who visited our house who had married a baron, so I had to curtsy to her instead of giving her a handshake. Her husband and eldest son had died in the war. She only had her youngest son left. He was away at Heidelberg University. I was usually bored and paid no attention to their conversation until one day, something caught my attention. The lady said, "In a few years, my son will be done with his studies and come back home. Brigitte would be a suitable wife. I would love to have grandchildren." That's when I had my "aha!" moment. I knew what they were up to—matchmaking.

I called it meddling. They had a lot of land. I never found out where the lady's money came from, but I secretly nicknamed her the "land baroness."

A few years later, the son was done at the university and dropped a bombshell. He came home and flew in with his little airplane—a small landing strip was on the premises—and said, "Hi mom, I have something to tell you. I changed my curriculum and I am now an ordained priest." I laughed so hard, and I'm sure God did too. After that, I referred to him as "the flying priest," the one that flew away! God played a joke on two meddling mothers.

Li'l Escape Artist!

Summer of 1967

We had bought a small ranch in October of 1966. It had a fenced-in yard, which was just what I was looking for. That'll keep a small child inside, right? In the summer of '68, we had bought a swing set with a slide, a children's picnic table with two benches, a sandbox, and a little kiddie pool. Everything a small child could want—except for a playmate.

Earlier that spring, we had met one of our neighbors. This was the same neighbor who helped translate my English. They had a three-year-old little girl named Lori.

We didn't own a TV, so my neighbor would invite my daughter Patty and I both over every morning at 8:00 a.m. to watch cartoons 'til 10:00 a.m. By 10:00 a.m., I would walk both girls back to my house to play outside and give them lunch. After that, it was nap time, and Lori's mom would come and take her home.

After that, I would sometimes go for a walk with them around the neighborhood. One day, Patty woke up early and she wanted to go to "Lori's house." I said no and to wait a while, for I had to use the bathroom. Patty was playing outside, so I decided not to disturb her and run in by myself really quick so I could use the restroom. With a four-foot chain-link fence, she was bound to be safe for a minute or two. The gate was locked. No problem. When I came back outside, she had disappeared.

At first, I thought she might play hide-and-seek or peek-a-boo with me. There was a large willow tree on the property. When I checked behind it, she wasn't there either. As I turned around, I saw her two little black shoes, neatly paired up with her little socks, tucked inside in front of the gate. Now I know what happened.

Her shoes didn't fit in chain-link spaces, so she took them off; her little toes fit. But...*where* is she? I panicked. We lived on Route 298, a truck route and across the street from a creek. A truck probably couldn't stop quickly enough if a child ran out in front of it. At the time that I was searching for

Patty, Mrs. Coville came out of her house. She was wondering where I was. She knew I would never allow her to come over by herself, especially not without footwear. Patty was with her. I then took Patty by her hand and asked her to show me which way she walked. There were no sidewalks and only gravel shoulders. She walked close to the houses over the lawns. She took the same way I showed her. She was a "creature of habit" and obedient. Smile.

She was also determined to go play with Lori when *she* wanted to, and nothing kept her from just doing that. I thanked God for watching over her.

A few years later, a six-year-old little boy ran out onto the street and was hit by a car. He was in critical condition. I never found out if he survived or not. The family moved away. I thanked God and the guardian angels again for keeping my child safe from harm, but I felt bad for the other family. My fears at that time were not unfounded.

Mother Knows Best!

1968

When my oldest daughter, Patty, was around two and a half years old, we went for a cook-out and swimming at the Green Lakes State Park. Patty stayed close to me. When we were done, I wrapped up scraps of leftovers in aluminum foil. I then took maybe five to six steps and put it in the garbage can. When I turned around, there was no Patty. She just seemed to have vanished into thin air. How can four adults lose a child in one minute or less?

Our friends from Switzerland came with us to the park—Tante Ruth and Onkel Hans. They ran toward the lifeguard stand. The lifeguard used his bullhorn and asked everyone to get out of the water. Only adults were asked to wade back in while holding hands, walking slowly, and feeling around with their feet for a little body. I had goosebumps all over. I panicked. My husband had joined the chain of people. I didn't. Just the thought of stumbling on her little body freaked me out.

I looked up and down the beach. I yelled at the lifeguards, "She's not in the water. Don't let anyone leave the parking lot." Fear gripped me. Oh God, please don't let her be kidnapped. The guards didn't listen to me, the mother. I didn't take the time to explain. I ran toward the parking lot. On the way, I passed a ladies restroom.

Earlier that day, I had taken her there because we both had to go potty. Now I knew exactly where she was. At two and a half, she was intrigued as to how a WC worked. You push a button and everything magically disappears. She did exactly what I did to her when she was done—to me. The only difference was she flushed before I was done. There were multiple stalls. I heard one toilet being flushed, then another, and another... I didn't see anyone coming out of the ladies' restroom. First, I looked underneath the doors. I didn't see any feet. So I slowly pushed each door open. No one. All of a sudden, I hear another flush and a womanly shriek, "Get her out of here!" Patty had crawled underneath all of the partitions, flushing one toilet after another. She also flushed the one with the lady still sitting on it. I started laughing, relieved that I found her.

When her father and the lifeguard saw us, they all wanted to know. "How did you know she was not in the water?" Simple: I didn't *see* her little black shoes on the beach close up to the water. She was neat and was told, "You don't wear your shoes into the water." They would have been neatly put there, side by side.

If you have ever just thought for a second that your child was gone, you know that fear you feel is *real*.

Thank God she was safe.

Where Is the Good Doctor When You Need Him?

In September 1968, when my oldest daughter, Patty, was three years old, my first husband and I decided to give her a future playmate. On March 10, 1969, I started to have labor pains three months early. Two weeks before that, the water had already broken. My doctor had advised me to stay in bed and take it easy, to "hang on" as long as possible to put a little more weight on her and hope her lungs mature. Now, that is easier said than done. Mother Nature had other plans.

My husband took me to the hospital. My labor pains were fifteen minutes apart but slowly, slowly went down to five. When the pains were only two minutes apart, I was wheeled into the delivery room. Now, surprisingly, the pains started to subside some and went back to being fifteen minutes apart again. I was wheeled into the hallway because another "customer" had arrived and was expected to deliver faster than I was. This happened two or three times. The doctor decided it was false labor, and he wanted to send me back home. I refused.

I said, "Oh no, you're not! There is nothing false about these pains." My sister was sent home once; she made it into her apartment, laid on the living room carpet, and had her baby alone, by herself. That also happened to me with my first child. She was two months early.

The ambulance driver put me in an elevator and said, "Good luck." That poor kid was nineteen years old, a PFC in the U.S. Army, scared to death, driving like a maniac. He said, "Please don't deliver before we get to the hospital. I've never delivered a baby. I've only seen it in a film in training."

You what? I was only twenty-one and had not even seen it on a film. Smile. When the elevator door opened, a nurse greeted me, got some information, and said, "All the delivery rooms are occupied. You have to wait here in the hallway. I'll go get you a chair." The pain was steady now. I looked around and saw an open bedroom door. The bed was empty. I waddled over, climbed into the bed, and had the baby before the nurse came back with her chair. So no, I am not going anywhere. I was wheeled back out into the hallway; it was some other lucky woman's turn.

Three resident doctors and nurses said, "You won't deliver today, we are now going to lunch. It is eleven. We'll be back by eleven-thirty. Then your doctor said to send you home. The baby is high and dry, there is no amniotic fluid left, she hasn't dropped into the birth canal and she's sideways. There is no way you are going to have this baby today."

Says who? My reply, of course. "I am not leaving. That baby is coming." And oh yes, she did. She made her debut into the world at 11:20 a.m., when I was laying on a gurney all by myself in the hallway. That also happened again twenty-two years later.

One of them said, "Guess you won't need an obstetrician, you'll need a pediatrician." No kidding, incubator and all.

The next day, one of the young doctors stopped by and apologized for leaving me all alone. He said one of them should have stayed with me. I said, "I told you I would deliver fast and my pains are not regular." I made a joke and said, "Oh, I know you read all about it in your medical books and you saw it in a movie."

He laughed and said, "No, but seriously, it was a miracle that the baby turned its head down first at the last second. Had she been breach, she most likely would have broken her neck." I am sure that young man turned out to be a caring, compassionate doctor with good bedside manners. In the delivery room, he said, "You can hold on to my arm and squeeze as hard as you want when the pains come—just don't bite me, and you are allowed to scream."

I only gnashed my teeth when the pain hit. I asked him if that would make the pain go away, he said no. I replied, "Then why bother."

Little Chicken

My second daughter was also a miracle baby. That is what I called her. She was born three months premature and weighed three pounds, two ounces and went down to two pounds, eleven ounces. She stopped breathing twenty-five times a day. Unbeknownst to me, she had an emergency baptism and her last rites at the same time. She was born in Saint Joseph's Hospital—Catholic—1969. They had just started to build a neonatal wing. It wasn't finished yet. There were two-by-fours with plastic sheets hanging on them, but they did have incubators where she stayed for two months. I was able to bring her home at five pounds. When she was born, she was unable to suck on a bottle. She had no eyebrows, no eyelashes, fingernails, toenails, hair, etc. Her skin was pale and the diapers too big.

All I could think of was that she looked like a little chicken in the supermarket. Her little arms looked like chicken wings, and her little ribcage stood out. After four weeks, the nurses improvised the diaper problem. They put a pink washcloth on her with those large diaper pins. Her eyes were covered with cotton balls for protection so the oxygen wouldn't cause harm. Well, this little chicken grew up to be a straight-A student, teaching deaf and hard-of-hearing children and is still teaching today in Los Angeles.

One time, she said to me, "Mom, I know why you called me a miracle baby. Some of the students I've worked with who were also premature and had complications during birth, like I did, have heart issues, lung problems, hearing loss, and sometimes vision loss.

Second Miracle for My "Miracle Baby"

May 1969

Finally, we were able to bring the baby home. She spent two months in the hospital. Her lungs had matured. She was strong enough to breathe on her own. There was never anything really wrong with her lungs. Breathing at being born three months early was just too hard for her at two pounds, eleven ounces. It tired her out, and she wasn't strong enough to take her next breath. We were overjoyed. Doctors have told us it would take at least three months, but there was just one little problem. She had to be fed every hour on the hour, 24/7, only one ounce per hour. She would suck only once or twice and fall back to sleep, so I had to tap her little feet to wake her back up. It took me forty-five to fifty minutes to feed her and give her a bath and ten minutes to boil more formula and diapers on the stove. (I didn't have a washer or dryer) I also had to make breakfast, lunch, and dinner for my four-year-old daughter, husband, and myself. I don't know how I did it, but I was determined to get that one ounce down her tummy. I never slept. I was a zombie, and it took its toll. After doing this for six weeks, I was bone tired—exhausted.

On a Friday night at midnight, I had just laid down for ten minutes when the baby started to cry. My husband was asleep next to me. Since he didn't have to go to work in the morning, I woke him up. I asked him if he could please get up and feed the baby. He refused. He said he needed his sleep... and I didn't??? I tried to get up but couldn't. Every time I tried to lift my head, I couldn't. I felt like I was sinking in a deep black hole. Sinking, sinking, sinking. I told him I couldn't. His answer: "Get up. You are the mother." And what did this "devoted father and husband" do? He pulled up his knees, put his feet on my back, and literally rolled me out of bed. I lay on the floor trying to sit up, then I passed out cold.

I came around about 6:00 a.m. There was no noise or movement in the bassinet. Now I was terrified the baby had died. I figured the crying had tired her out so much that she couldn't take her next breath. I was paralyzed with fear and couldn't move. I lay on the floor unable to move for at least an hour.

I didn't want to know for sure. I'd rather not know. As long as I didn't know, I could still cling to the hope she was alive. I prayed "Dear God, please, please let her be alive." I couldn't get up, even though I wanted to.

I finally forced myself to get up and look in the bassinet. To my relief, she was sound asleep. That was the first time I hated my husband with a passion. Somehow, I felt he was punishing the baby to get back at me for something I might have done or something I might have not done. I just couldn't figure it out. When we got married, he said he wanted six children to show the world he can be "productive." He just didn't want to take care of them on a daily basis. He only played with them when it was convenient. I thanked God that the baby was alive. It truly was a miracle. She had missed at least seven feedings. I made a promise to myself not to have another child with him… and I didn't. I went on the birth-control pill. That infuriated him. I also vowed to leave him as soon as the baby was out of diapers. I didn't go through with it—not yet. That came a little later.

He asked me to join a wife-swapping group. I said, "No, go by yourself." I didn't want to be passed around like an old worn-out shoe. I didn't get married for that. And that from a former altar boy. He said he couldn't go alone; he needed a wife. I replied, "Find another one." He did.

Failed Suicide

August 1969

A few months later, we moved to another house that only had two bedrooms. The old one had three bedrooms but no basement, attic, or garage. It was in a nice neighborhood; sidewalks for the girls to roller skate and ride the bicycles on. Church was four houses down the road, and the Catholic school was basically in our backyard. They could slip through the fence and walk to school without having to cross the street. I could watch them walk there through my kitchen window. It was idealistic for the girls, but I had been unhappy for a long time. I always felt he didn't love me. He just married me to have children. I had the impression he really didn't care who the mother was. He just treated me like a household appliance. He could put me on the shelf when needed; as long as he had clean clothes, dinner on the table, and the kids were taken care of, he was happy. As long as he could pursue his hobbies—flying, playing golf, tennis, and soft-ball with his coworkers—he was happy: All that on a seventy-one-dollar-a-week take-home pay. My bank account in Germany dwindled away rapidly. There were times I didn't eat because I had to make sure he and the girls had enough. He never noticed I wasn't eating. He never noticed anything. I had started to work in a sleeping bag company in Syracuse. One day, something lodged into my eye—a small speck from the filling. It scratched my eye every time I blinked. I went to the nurse. She put gauze and a black eye patch over my right eye. My husband picked me up from work. The car had a bench seat, and I would always sit close to him, but that day, I didn't. He said nothing and neither did I. I was waiting for him to ask me what had happened. Nothing. He hadn't even notice. How could he not? He never really looked at me.

 The second time, he had gone to Illinois on a ten-day business trip. He had a promotion—sales and marketing. He was in a tent, promoting their product. He worked for Franklin Engine Co. which was based in Liverpool, New York. At one time, they manufactured cars and helicopter engines for the U.S. Army. The Vietnam War was going on, so helicopters were being shot down and business was booming. When he had left for the trip, I had long brown hair with black and blonde streaked curls on the top on my head. When he returned, I had short black hair. He didn't notice. Well, after three days, he said, "Somehow you look different. I just can't figure out what it is." At least that was an improvement. I was impressed. Not.

I already felt unloved plus the post-partum depression set in—not enough to eat or sleep. I didn't want to live anymore. I was only twenty-six years old. Since I always knew that my mother didn't want or love me, I felt I was unlovable. As a child, I entertained the thought that "when I grow up and get married, I will finally have someone who loves me." Yeah right. I was, and still am, an incurable romantic. I didn't know people married for convenience, money, or some ulterior motive. I thought you married for love. I was naïve.

One Saturday afternoon, I did the unthinkable; I tried to kill myself. I thought sleeping pills would be the best way to do it. I would die in my sleep, painlessly. The problem was, I didn't have any. I asked my husband to go around the corner to the drug store to buy me some sleeping pills. He did. Just like always, he was clueless. He said he was going to take the girls to a matinee Walt Disney movie that ran from 2:00 p.m. to 4:00 p.m. As soon as he left, I sat down and wrote my suicide note, swallowed the whole bottle of pills, and went to bed. I didn't know that the pills didn't have barbiturates in them nor did I even know what that word meant.

I had gone to bed maybe thirty minutes or so when my husband came in the door and tried to wake me up. I was groggy and just talked incoherently. He went to the movie theater but forgot his wallet and had to come home. Was it a coincidence? Was it a miracle? I believe three miracles happened that day: The first are the pills didn't have barbiturates in them; the second, my husband forgot his wallet; and the third is that he came back in time. It wasn't my time to go.

After he found me, he took me to the hospital. The doctors said I had to stay so they could observe my progress. He said, "No, I need her home to take care of the children." The doctors won. On Wednesday, he visited and wanted to bring his laundry to clean with the washer and dryer at the hospital. The nurses threw him out. He had no concern for me or my well-being.

The Fifth Miracle

1969

My first husband, Richard, decided he wanted a little private airplane—a small Piper Cub, a two-seater. After he had his license, he asked me to go for little flight with him. By then, we had two little girls. We had a neighbor watch the two girls. When we arrived at the little airport in Cicero, New York, he said he wanted to fuel up. No attendees were around; the pumps were locked. I asked him if we had enough fuel to go ahead. He said, "Yes." So, we headed up in the air over Oneida Lake. Next to the lake, there was Highway 81. There were also high power lines with a red ball. Ten minutes later, up in the air, the engine stopped.

I said to Richard, "Turn the engine on."

He said "I can't."

I replied "Can't or won't? If you're trying to scare me, you've succeeded, so turn the engine back on."

He said, "I can't—we're out of fuel. I thought we had at least fifteen minutes of flight time, but don't worry, I'll put the nose down—that'll get the propeller going."

I closed my eyes and prayed, "Dear God, please don't let us land in the lake, on top of a car, or on a high voltage wire." By the grace of God, we made a safe landing. I never set foot in the little plane again.

Is There a Lifeguard on Duty?

On a nice summer day in 1970, my daughter Patricia and I went swimming at the Green Lakes State Park. She was only five years old at that time. Carla was only one year old, taking a nap. We decided to leave Dad and the little one home and go by ourselves, only the "big girls." After we've spent a good amount of time in the water, Patricia had enough of Mom's swimming lessons and wanted to play on the beach with her sand toys. So we sort of camped out behind the lifeguard stand. After a while, Patty moved around a bit and somehow ended up in front of the lifeguard stand. I didn't think anything of it and just watched her play happily and content. I also watched other children play in the water.

Soon, I noticed some older boys dunking some younger children. I figured maybe they were siblings and just fooling around. After a few minutes, I realized that the older boys dunked the smaller ones way too long. I brought it to the young lifeguard's attention. He wasn't paying attention. He was busy talking to his friends. Then he saw that these smaller children were dunked dangerously long, the older boys seemed to enjoy it when the little ones came up sputtering water and grasping for air. They were clearly distressed. The lifeguard recognized the danger, jumped off the stand, but he didn't walk down the steps, he didn't look down, he just kept his eyes on the children in the water. He never even realized that he jumped on top of my daughter. He took off like a loose cannon. Patty's head was in the sand face down. I picked her up, and what I saw made my heart stop a beat. One side of her face was covered in blood. It came gushing out, her long hair plastered on one side of her face. All I could think was, *Dear God, not her eye, please don't let her lose an eye.* I was in panic mode. I grabbed her, the car keys, and a towel only. I left blankets and sand toys behind. I laid her on the front seat and gunned it out of the parking lot.

It was only one and a half miles to the Village of Minoa, New York, right on Main Street where two doctors' offices were. It was a Saturday, and I hoped that they had special hours for people who couldn't make it from Monday to Friday between eight and five. The first one was Dr. Bishop's house. I ran over the curb and sidewalk onto the front lawn. I jumped out of the car, knocked on the door—nothing. I got behind the wheel again, driving with my left hand, and pressed the towel with my right hand over her eye to stop the bleeding. About four houses down was Doctor Carhardt's office. I didn't bother to back out onto the road; I just drove on the front lawn to his office. No luck there either.

Now, I really panicked. The nearest hospital was in downtown Syracuse, New York, approximately fifteen to twenty miles away. I didn't know how to get there. I raced to my house, left the car running, ran inside, and yelled, "Richard, Richard, take Patty to the ER. She is in the car bleeding. I think she is losing her eye."

He was watching TV. Usually, his eyes were glued to the screen, and he paid no attention to what I said. This time, though, he jumped right up and ran out the door. The urgency in my voice and my state of mind must have told him it must be something serious. He never asked, "What, where or how," and his usual "Oh, you are just overreacting." I sort of collapsed onto the couch, relieved he was taking over.

Three hours later, they came back. When the lifeguard had jumped onto her back and pushed her face into the sand, the impact had split her skin just above the eyebrow, but her eye was fine. Had there been a stone or toy in the sand, she could have lost her eye. Thank God there wasn't. She only needed two or three stitches. Someone was watching out for her. Until today, I never go near a lifeguard stand. Having a lifeguard on duty gives parents a false sense of security. They are not watching. For some strange reason, I always seem to be watching other children.

What I am telling you next has nothing to do with miracles; it's just to stress my point to parents—"lifeguards do not watch." When I had my second dry-cleaning establishment in a high-rise apartment building, it had a large swimming pool. I kept Saturday hours. One Saturday, I took my girls and my nephew Lee with me. He was living with me at that time. I was only open from 8:00 a.m. to noon. I kept them busy with books, puzzles, etc. in the back of the store, then we went swimming. Little Lee was five years old. Older kids were showing off, making somersaults, etc. off the diving board. The little guy kept begging me to let him jump off the diving board. At first, I said no, but then I gave in and said yes. He was a little charmer and begged so nicely.

Well, I watched him jump. He went down to the bottom and just sat there, blowing bubbles. He never tried to propel himself up. I looked at the lifeguard on the opposite side of the pool, expecting him to jump in and get him up. And what was the lifeguard doing? Reading a book! So I dove in myself and brought him up.

I asked him, "Lee, why didn't you come up and swim over to where I was?"

His answer. "I don't know how to swim. I just wanted to jump. I knew you would come and get me." Out of the mouths of babes.

The next incident happened twenty-plus years later. My friends were visiting from Germany. We took them to Niagara Falls and over to Canada. On top of our hotel was a large pool with a slide, taller than I had ever seen at that time or since. By then, I had an in-ground pool at my house with a small slide—no diving board. My youngest daughter, Jennifer, was only two and a half years old, a good swimmer. When she asked me if she could go down the slide, I said yes. There was a long line; I didn't want to go with her. I sat on the edge of the pool and watched the other kids slide down. After a long wait, the kids, of course, were over-anxious when it was their turn. They came speeding down like bullets, one right after the other, practically on top of each other. They didn't wait for the others ahead of them to come up and swim out of the way. Parents, what parents? It seems like they were all sleeping in. After all, a lifeguard was on duty to keep law and order, right? When it was my daughter's turn, I got up and yelled up to the child on top, "Don't come down yet, stay put until she comes up and swims out of reach." Surprisingly, that child actually listened to me. My little one was only two and a half years old, lighter than the rest, and seemed to come down even faster than the rest, straight down to the bottom. She sat there motionless, not reacting as usual. She seemed dazed. The speed and depth had knocked the wind out of her.

I looked at the lifeguard. Ah, yes, your friendly pool guy. He had his back turned, picking up wet towels, putting them in a large wheeled hamper, reaching for another one, and putting dry folded towels on a rack. Not much help coming from him. After I stared at my baby for a few seconds, I jumped in myself. By the time I got to her, her survival instinct had kicked in; she pushed herself off the floor and started to go up, but it was too deep. I knew she would never make it up to the surface in time on her own. So I grabbed her and sped things up. Thank God that child on top had listened and waited until we were out of reach for her to land on our heads and push us down again before we had a chance to catch another breath. Again, it wasn't our time yet.

Oh, and one other thing. Another hotel, another pool, another lifeguard. Mother Nature called, he went to the restroom. At the time, I thought, *Why wasn't he told never to leave the pool? Call another hotel employee to take over for a few minutes? Those few minutes could save a life.* God entrusted us with the precious life of *his* children to keep them safe. They are *ours* for just a little while.

The Little Wanderer/Wanderlust

August 1970

It was a nice hot summer Saturday afternoon. I wanted to go shopping. Usually, I always took the girls with me. My first husband, Richard, at that time volunteered to babysit his children. It was a rare occasion for me to go anywhere except to work by myself. So I left. When I came back an hour and a half later, I got out of the car and looked around for my girls. I only saw my oldest, Patty, on the sidewalk. I looked around for her father, but I didn't see Carla, who was only eighteen months at the time. I thought, *Surely, he didn't leave her alone in the house? You just don't leave an eighteen-month old alone.* But it was far worse. He was across the street, sitting on the front porch with the neighbor. I walked over there and asked, "Where is Carla?"

He answered, "I don't know."

How many times can my poor heart stop? I looked up and down the street, porches, and backyards, but there was no sign of her. I panicked. Just then, a car pulled up beside me. A lady got out, walked around the car to the passenger door, and said, "I found someone in front of McMahon's grocery store. I recognized her and knew just who she belonged to and where to bring her." She opened the car door, and my little Carla sat in the seat, sound and safe. I was so relieved and thankful. I didn't personally know her, but everyone in the village (Minoa, New York) knew me. Smile.

I was a cashier in the only supermarket, too small to be called that, but it had everything you needed. If you wanted lobster, scallops, crab legs, snails, etc., you had to go to Syracuse. Everyone in the village stopped there at least once a week. I was the cahier with the accent. In the evening and on weekends, I would take my girls for a walk—summers in a stroller, winter on a sled.

So people saw me with my girls and knew who they belonged to—well, who the mother was anyway. I walked one mile each way to and from work. Sometimes someone would recognize me, stop, and give me a ride. One lady took it one step further. She saw me walking in a snowstorm. She asked me what my hours were. I told her Monday through Friday, nine to six. From then on, she stopped by the store every day at six, just buying fresh meat, sausage, etc. She never bought frozen meat. The lady was Dr. Bishop's wife. She did notice my husband's car was in the driveway. It was embarrassing.

He never picked up the girls from our neighbors nor did he pick me up from work. All he did was watch TV. Heaven forbid if I ever should have asked him to set the table or boil a potato. He came home an hour before I quit work at six and then walked one mile home. Sometimes, someone would give me a ride in the morning. That is why everyone knew my girls, myself, and where I lived. This eighteen-month-old little girl toddled across one side street two blocks to a five-lane intersection on busy Main Street. My little smarty took the same route I took when I took them to McMahon's for ice cream, popsicles, etc. She stayed on the sidewalk. It truly was a miracle she wasn't run over by a car or truck or taken by a stranger, pedophile, killer, human trafficker, etc. I am convinced her guardian angel held her hand and was with her until God sent the right lady, at the right time, to bring her home at the same time I arrived home also.

The village part-time police chief also lived close by. If he had found her, whether he knew me or not, he and his wife also gave me a ride home once in a while, I am sure he would have had CPS involved. It would have been his duty to report it. The very least that could have happened was that we lost custody of both girls. I don't think I would have survived a broken heart.

After that, I didn't let their father watch them by himself; a sitter or a mom was close by. After we were separated, I lost control when he took the girls by himself. One Sunday afternoon, Richard and his girlfriend Kathy, his second wife, picked up both girls. He said he'd be back in two and a half hours. He dropped off his dirty clothes. I did his laundry on Sundays. When he asked me to iron his shirt, sew on buttons, etc., I quit. Let the girlfriend do it. After that, his visitations became less regular to say the least. Before he brought back the girls, my neighbor burst into my house yelling at me and was furious. I had no idea what hit me. She screamed, "How can you possibly drop off a seven- and three-year-old in a movie theater by themselves?" I was shocked. I convinced her that I was home during this time, the girls are with their dad, and I had no idea they were at the movies, and they are still not home. What happened was that their father and his girlfriend dropped them off at the theater and left. The movie was *Bambi*. When Bambi was shot,

Carla cried, got up, and left. When she didn't return, my neighbor got up, and when she couldn't find her in the lobby or both restrooms, thank god she had a mother's instinct and looked outside. She found three year old Carla wandering around the parking lot trying to decide which way to walk home.

Fayetteville, New York, has Erie Canal close by and Route 5; that spells *danger*. He and his girlfriend wanted time to themselves. I took him to family court, and the judge decided he didn't deserve to see his children but only for six months.

Coincidence again? My neighbor taking her own two children to the same theater on the same day at the same time, sitting behind my girls. If she had sat in front of them, she wouldn't have noticed. She went outside looking for Carla at the right time before something tragic happened. The angels and God were with her; no one just has that much luck. Somewhere I read the only tragedy in life is not to know God. So don't worry about anything else. Of course, to have known him and then ignore him could be worse. My opinion. And no, no one asked me for it. (Smile.)

James Street Miracle

1972

Two years later, I had a small dry cleaning and laundry business, and I also did alterations. My oldest daughter, Patricia, six at the time, had a dance recital. My husband, the girls, and I were to meet at 2:00 p.m. at a school. I had to go to work at 8:00 a.m. to open up my little store in the bottom of the skyline apartments on James Street in Syracuse. Well, James Street has a somewhat steep decline. I put my foot on the brake to slow down, but nothing happened. I pumped and pumped the brakes, going faster and faster. Then, to my right, I saw a city bus. I panicked and swerved side to side to slow the car down. There was no oncoming traffic nor pedestrians on the sidewalk as I went on curbs, sidewalks, grass, buildings, etc. When the car finally came to a stop, I was shaking, my heart pounding, and I just slumped over the steering wheel, eyes closed. Before I could compose myself, there was a knock on the window. A policeman stood there with a pen and ticket booklet and asked me to roll down the window. I automatically obeyed and he said, "Tell me, how did you get around the telephone pole?"

I said, "What telephone pole?"

He continued, "How did you get around the mailbox?"

And I said, "What mailbox?"

"How did you get around a fire hydrant?"

"What fire hydrant?"

"How did you manage to avoid colliding into the brick building?"

I was shaking like a leaf in the wind. I finally stammered "I have no brakes!"

When he said, "Get out of the car," my knees buckled, and he had to hold me up. He walked me inside my little store, put me in a chair, and said, "Stay put. I'll get you some coffee." At 2:00 p.m., I went to the dance recital.

My husband said "What's wrong with you? You're white as a sheet and shaking? Did a ghost walk over your grave?"

I answered, "I almost killed myself today!" Before I could continue, he held up his hand and said, "Wait, don't tell me. Let me guess—you had no brakes."

I was shocked! I couldn't believe what I was hearing. I said, "You mean to tell me you knew?"

He said, "I started to take out your old brake shoes, they need replacing, but it got dark, so I didn't put the new ones in. I forgot to tell you. Next time, don't go down a hill, go up or around the hill." What a prince of a guy. You just gotta love that man.

My reply was "Why don't you divorce me instead of killing me?"

I hadn't had time to pray as I frantically turned the wheel from side to side. My guardian angel and God had to have a hand in that. Even the policeman said it was a miracle that there wasn't any traffic or pedestrians on the sidewalk, that I missed the building and could've crashed into the hydrant, etc., or killed yourself. Now, as I see it, it was eight multiple miracle. That was when my life was spared again. I finally wanted a divorce, and my husband said, "Your dreamboat turned into a 'garbage barge.'" Yes, my "ship" came in, but then it "sunk" in the Harbor. Life goes on. We both remarried.

Blood Poisoning

1972

Since I always prayed for my children's guardian angels to keep them safe, and I still do, I guess Carla kept them a little busy also. When she was three years old, she went down the basement stairs to watch cartoons. She had her breakfast plate in her hand. She slipped and hit her face on the step. She had a tiny cut above her upper lip. It wasn't very wide, but I thought it might be a little deeper than just a scratch. My neighbor was a nurse, so I took her next door to have the neighbor take a look at it. I asked her if I should take her to the doctor and maybe get at least two stitches. She said no and that I should just "butterfly" it with a Band-Aid and she would be fine. It was a Friday. I put her on the bus for her pre-K school. I figured that if the school nurse thought it was something to be concerned about, she would give me a call. Everything seemed to be fine. She came home, had dinner, played with her older sister, watched cartoons, had her nightly bath, and we said our prayers. I sang my nightly lullaby in German and lay down for a while with each girl until they went to sleep. Lights out! Just like any other evening.

In the morning, Carla didn't get up like she usually did. I went into her room to check and see what the matter was. She was as white as a sheet, listless, almost lethargic. The cut on her lip was slightly swollen, and a red streak went up toward her eye. I knew what it was. It was blood poisoning and it was very dangerous. My mother almost died from it when I was six years old. I took my older daughter to a neighbor and rushed Carla to the emergency room. That is where my nightmare began. I told the ER doctor what happened. She fell down the stairs; she did not tumble, only slipped on one stair. He asked me who her pediatrician was. I gave him the name. It was the same doctor who discharged her three years or earlier from the hospital when she finally weighed five pounds. I went to his office for her six-week and six-month checkup; that was only two times I took her. At first, they could not get a hold of him, but he did confirm that I had been seen by him only two times. That seemed to ring an alarm with the doctor.

He kept on questioning me, only his voice and demeanor had changed. Now it was more like an interrogation. He shot his questions so fast at me I had hardly time to answer.

"Does she always fall down?"

"No."

"Has she been seen by other doctors?"

"No."

"Why not?" I don't know, she was never sick.

"What about her shots, did you get all of her immunizations?"

"Yes."

"How? You never took her to a doctor?"

"I took her to the clinic in East Syracuse."

"When? Do you have the papers to prove it?"

"Yes. At home."

"Can anyone verify it?"

"Yes. My neighbor and his little girl went with me."

"What's his name? Address? Phone number?"

They called, but he was a break man for the railroad on his way to Albany. The next thing I knew, a lady came into the room. She introduced herself and said she was from the Child Protection Services (CPS). At that time, I had no idea what exactly that was. I was just scared stiff. I didn't speak fluent English. Sometimes I reverted back to German and stuttered. The next thing I knew, two policemen showed up. The doctors and the CPS obviously thought I abused and neglected my child. At that time, they had not spoken to the pediatrician nor my neighbor. Cell phones hadn't been invented yet. They pretty much asked the same questions.

"Do you ever hit your child? Did you push her down the stairs? We know you did."

"No, I wasn't near her."

"Where were you? Do you often leave the girls alone?"

No matter what I said, I had a feeling they did not believe a word. The ER doctor came back in and said, "The blood poisoning is getting worse. The red streak is only two to three millimeters away from the brain. This can cause irreversible brain damage or result in death. The antibiotics are not working, we need to make an incision and need your signature." I signed. The sooner the better.

Now, the doctor said, "Where is her dad?"
I answered, "I don't know. We were recently separated."
"Do you have legal custody?"
"No, we haven't gone to court yet." Now the police got involved.
"What's his name? Where does he live?"
"I don't know."
"What's his phone number?"
"I don't know, he never said."
"What kind of car does he drive?"

I told him what the license plate number was. I had heard from someone else that they had seen his car parked somewhere on Salina Street in downtown Syracuse. The police went looking for him. They found him and brought him in to sign the papers. I was by the gurney holding my little girls lifeless hand. I asked him to stand on the other side and hold her other little hand. He did for a minute or so and he said he had to go. His girlfriend, Kathy, was sitting in the car in the hospital parking lot. They were on their way to go bowling. He was on her team. He left.

The doctor and the policeman looked at each other in disbelief. I was shocked. All I could say to them was, "And that is the father whose signature you required? Wasting precious time locating him and risking brain damage or death?" The antibiotics finally worked; she didn't need the incision after all. I didn't understand why a mother's signature wasn't efficient enough. They never asked the father any questions.

Carla was kept overnight. I wanted to stay by her side and stay in the hospital with her. The nurses said I couldn't and that I had to leave. About half a mile from the hospital, I ran out of gas. So I had to walk twenty miles to go home. Back then, there was a gasoline shortage. You can only get gas according to your license plate numbers. Even numbers could get gas on even days, and odd numbers on odd days. It wasn't my day. I had to walk home in the dark. It was raining. The next day, I got up early to go back to the hospital. Thankfully, my neighbor drove me back to my car.

A few months later, Carla's dad asked if he could move back home and try again. I said no. "Any father who chooses bowling over a sick child does not deserve to have one." I hated him for that.

Everything turned out well for her. She was mostly a grade A student and went on to become a teacher for students who are deaf and hard of hearing in

Los Angeles, where she is still teaching today. She has touched a lot of children's lives. What a tragedy it would have been if she had brain damage or had died. God had a different plan for her. It wasn't her time. God and the angels watched over her for the second time. But it wasn't the last time.

Will the Owner Please Call the Police?

1974 or 1975

At the time I had the small dry cleaning, laundry, and alterations business on James Street, I also had a second one in another high-rise apartment building near Upstate Medical Center. I can't remember the name of the street. A nearby hotel, I think it was a Holiday Inn, had a comedy show on the top floor. So I stayed in town one night, and I left there at about 10:00 p.m., got on I-690, and headed home. It was winter; a typical Syracuse blizzard was raging. I could hardly see anything. The roads were icy. I don't remember why I slammed on the brakes. I did several doughnuts, spinning out of control, and ended up on the right-hand shoulder and hit a large metal pole, *head on!* The car was an old Chevy Belair; it didn't have seat belts back then. After I composed myself and realized I wasn't hurt, I heard and felt a large crash. The large green metal sign, indicating the next exits, fell on the roof of the car.

First, I threw myself onto the bench seat. I still heard small crunching noises. I looked up and saw that the car roof was slowly being crushed down, caving from the weight of the sign. I knew I had to get out of there in a hurry. God and what to do!

I tried to open the door, but it wouldn't budge. Panic set in. Now what? The old car windows were manual back then. I rolled down the window; it only went halfway down. I threw out my purse, then wiggled myself out headfirst. I looked at the car. The hood looked like an accordion, the tires and tire rims were square, the back of the car stood up like a fish tail. I climbed over the guardrails, and walked to a bowling alley and called a friend to take me home. The next morning, I saw a photo of my car in the newspaper. They must have gotten some information from my license plate because they knew it was a woman. Police found an abandoned car, no sign of the woman, no accident report, and no one admitted to a hospital. "Will the owner please contact the police?" I did. They were worried I might have been buried in a snow bank. My guardian angels were at work again!

The Second Husband

Approximately 1975

My second husband, Harold, cheated on me almost from the start. Everyone at work knew it but me. The wife is almost always the last to know. Then one day, a man at work said to him, "While you're out chasing all these women, you leave your wife home alone. What do you think she is doing all this time you're not there?" I am sure the man didn't imply that I was cheating, he just gave him food for thought, a hint to stay home. After that, he became insanely jealous. Just because he cheated on me, he assumed I was doing the same. One night after work, there was a blizzard, a total white-out. I drove home very slow and careful, five to ten miles per hour. So naturally, I wasn't home on time. Duh. His guilty mind thought that I was with another man. He set out looking for me.

On my way home, there is a few miles of nothing but railroad tracks on one side from East Syracuse to Minoa. Just one or two repair shops, closed of course, no houses, etc.—a deserted road. This part of the railroad was used to "bump" the railroad cars onto different tracks to go to their assigned destination. All of a sudden, a car came up behind me and hit my rear bumper. I tried to go faster to get away and put some distance between the cars.

All of a sudden, a car passed me on the left at high speed and put on the brakes in front of me. I realized then that it was my husband, Harold. He spun to the right into a ditch. I slammed on my brakes, but pumped several times, made a few doughnuts, and finally stopped. I looked back, but there was no movement in his car. So what do I do? Just what any loving wife would do! I got out of the car and walked back to his car to see if he was hurt, needed medical attention, or just a tow truck. Halfway there, his car door opened, and he came charging toward me like a raging bull! He was 6'3" and weighed 225 pounds. I immediately turned around, trying to get back inside my car and lock the door, but no such luck!

I didn't have a chance to open my door. He grabbed my head between his large hands, comparable to bear paws, and repeatedly slammed the back of my head on the hood of my car. My brain felt scrambled, and the back of my head felt like mush. I was afraid he would kill me. Then, out of nowhere, I thought I heard someone say, "Play dead." I called it an angel whisper. I immediately closed my eyes, relaxed my whole body, and just slid into the snow.

And what does this loving husband do? He takes off! He thought he had killed me. There were no witnesses. It probably would remain an "unsolved mystery." I drove home, and his car wasn't there; surprise, surprise! The cowardly lion thought the police would be there to arrest him. My house was just five houses away from a small annex police station which was later on dissolved and merged with the Manlius, New York police department. I wasn't able to sleep on my back for weeks. My skull, the bones, felt like rubber. He showed up a few days later, said he was so, so sorry and that if I went to the police, he wouldn't blame me. I decided not to press charges. Big mistake. Love is blind and marriage is an eye opener. Smile.

The straw that broke the camel's back was a little later. My neighbor, Lucille, was Italian, and one day, she asked me if I wanted to go to a potluck dinner near the Syracuse University at a church near Nottingham. I can't recall the exact name, but it was something like "The Foreign Wives Club." It mostly consisted of foreign students' wives from resident doctors at the university teaching hospital, upstate medical, research doctors, etc. My neighbor didn't have a driver's license or a car at that time. She asked me to be ready two hours earlier. She forgot to mention that she had volunteered to set up the folding tables and chairs.

On the way there, she also said, "Oh, by the way, can we pick up my sister? She doesn't drive either." After that, we went there, set up everything and put the large restaurant-sized oven on warm. All the ladies brought a dish from their home country: Italy, Iran, France, and my German dish. Some of the ladies also performed a dance from their country. When it was over, I got ready to leave. My neighbor said, "Oh, I forgot to tell you. My sister signed up with the cleanup committee."

I had no choice but to also help speed things up. We finally arrived back in my driveway around midnight. I noticed the basement light was not on when we left but was on now. No car in the driveway either.

She said, "Do you want me to come in with you?"

I answered, "No, go on home. I probably just forgot." I went to the kitchen, opened the basement door, and started to go down the basement stairs. Halfway down, I *froze*. There was my husband, sitting on the couch with a hunting rifle draped over his knees. I could tell he was *drunk*. He started interrogating me. Where have you been? Who was the guy? I know you are cheating on me. etc., etc. I tried to explain where I was. Does it sound as if there are men in a wives' club? Duh! I explained about the setup and cleanup committee. I told him to go ask my neighbor. He was too drunk to get up. Round and round, over and over, questioning me about the same thing. By 6:00 a.m., standing, arguing, and making him understand I did nothing wrong, I felt drained and exhausted. I figured as long as I keep him talking, he might sober up. I silently kept praying, "Dear God, don't let that thing be loaded, and thank you, God, my girls are not home." They were at Lou's house.

Finally, something said in my head, "Use psychology and prey on his weaknesses."

So, I said, "Harold, if you kill me, you are the first person the police will be looking for. When you go to jail, there will be no more pot, whiskey, and women. You'll probably be someone's 'girlfriend.'" Those possibilities obviously sobered him up. Very slowly, he unloaded the rifle, six bullets one at a time. I couldn't believe it. I asked him where his car was. He said around the corner, in front of the police station. Huh? How drunk can you get! He might as well have left a calling card.

Sometimes You See It Coming, Sometimes You Don't!

Around the year 1975, I had a supervisory position in a warehouse. Since I was the "new kid on the block," I was put on the afternoon shift—3:00 p.m.–11:00 p.m. It was the "unfavorable shift." All the guys wanted to be home in the evening so that they could go bowling and do other things.

My daughter, Carla, was around six years old at the time and Patty, ten. The babysitter lived only four houses up the street on the same side as us, with a sidewalk to connect the houses. Carla had been told to never call me at work unless it was an emergency. An "emergency" has a different meaning to a six-year-old mind.

Carla wanted to know if she and Patty could walk down the street, go home, and sleep in my king-sized bed so we could all wake up together in the morning and have pillow fights. This was around 9:00 p.m. on a Friday night. I had Saturday off. I hesitated. The sitter came on the phone and said, "I will walk them down and make sure they go to bed." So, I agreed; a decision that could have haunted me for the rest of my life. I don't think I could have gotten over it.

At about 10:30 p.m., the phone rang again. It was Carla. She was half crying and said, "Patty ruined your down-blanket from Germany. Now she is afraid she is in trouble. Is she?"

I answered, "Well, I'll see when I get home." I figured, how bad could it be? Maybe they took some cookies or a drink to bed and spilled it. They had never done this. It was one of the rules I enforced like my oma. But...oh my god, I was not prepared for what I saw when I walked into my bedroom. I fell on my knees and hugger her. I was overwhelmed with relief and gratitude. Thank god they were both alive! Who cared about a blanket?

That was one accident I didn't see coming. Next to my bed was a nightstand. Patty had fallen asleep and obviously tossed and turned, getting an arm entangled in the cord of the lamp. She had pulled the lamp on her chest, close to her face and long hair. The lampshade, a "clip-on," came off. The hot lightbulb burned or, should I say, melted a large hole in the blanket.

Miraculously, it did not catch on fire, and neither did her nightgown or long hair. I had a duvet cover over the blanket. The top cover was silk jacquard and underneath was a thick real linen cover to prevent the fluffy little feather-puffs to poke through. I was so shook up. If I didn't believe in God, angels, and miracles already, then that night would have made a "believer" out of me.

The nightstand and bed had been eleven years old. The girls' father was six foot two inches with long arms. All of this happened on *his* side of the bed. Nothing had ever happened like this before. So *no*, I did not see it coming. If they both had perished in a fire, I don't know how I could have gone on living with the knowledge that I gave them permission. The guilt would have surely killed me. Praise the Lord. I probably would have set myself on fire. I loved these two little girls with all of my heart. I was supposed to keep them safe and protect them from accidents like these; anticipated disaster, keeping the house "child-proof."

What Is a Hurricane?

I was about to find out...
Today is March 8, 2018. Last evening, I had remembered something else. It comes all in bits and pieces. If God had let me remember everything at once, it would have been too overwhelming. All of a sudden, when I was just drifting off to sleep... "Camping, Nova Scotia"—that was all that came to mind. I was too sleepy to get up and jot down a headline. All I said to myself was, *Please, God, let me remember in the morning.* I did.

***

I think it was the end of August in 1977, maybe 1978. One of my neighbors and babysitters told me that she and her husband went camping in Nova Scotia and had a good time. I had never been camping before, so I thought it was a good idea and wanted to give it a try. I had no equipment, though. A girlfriend at work said I could borrow her tent and little camping stove.

I also had a friend who used to collect rents from rental properties. He said he would go with the girls and I. I said, "All right!" I was a little afraid of venturing out by myself. The girls went to bed early because we wanted to leave early in the morning. My friend called around 10:00 p.m. and said, "Why don't you let your neighbor watch the girls and you and I go by ourselves?"

I said, "Okay, no problem." I hung up the phone, woke up my girls, packed the car, locked the house, and left at one in the morning, hours before he was due. There was no way I was going to leave my girls behind. I had promised them a vacation to Nova Scotia, and that is what they got.

It was a trip to remember for all of the wrong reasons. First, I got lost near Boston. I drove around in a big loop three times, each of them being one hour worth of time. All of a sudden, I heard a police car siren and saw flashing lights. The policeman said, "I've been watching you drive around for three hours. Do you know where you want to go? Are you lost?" Duh. Wasn't that obvious? I told him I wanted to go to Portland, Maine, catch a cruise ship, and sail to Nova Scotia. Well, now I had a police escort showing me the way. How embarrassing!

I arrived close to the harbor early in the morning. I took a room at the nearest motel with a swimming pool. I needed some sleep and the girls could go swimming. The departing time was not until 10:00 p.m.

Now, when I had made the reservation, they had asked me if I wanted a berth, but what I understood was "birth." I didn't know what that meant. It didn't make sense to me. I didn't want to admit that I had no idea what that was. I was a grown woman; a world-traveler. We ended up sleeping on the floor cushions in a lounge on the ship. Yeah—pride will get you everywhere except getting you a berth.

Now, before we departed in Nova Scotia, a young kid, eighteen, asked me if he could have a ride to a college. He said he was a student. As we rolled off the ship, Canadian border control stopped each car, checked drivers licenses, car registration, passports, etc. They didn't bother to check him. I didn't think of the dangers of picking up a hitchhiker. I was naïve. In the '50s and '60s, it was common for students to hitchhike all over Europe, so I didn't think anything of it. The words pedophile, rapist, ax-murderer, serial-killer, etc., were foreign to me. I had never heard of them. But…that wasn't the case.

This kid harbored a different secret. I had agreed to drive him to the college. It was out of my way, but hey, the whole island is only ninety-miles wide. I could make that in one hour—no big detour. At one time, he asked me to stop near a farm. I asked him why. He said he wanted to look for work. We were still miles away from the college he wanted to go to. I told him it was too far away. That is when he took off his cap, pointed to his shaved head, and said, "I lied to you. I am not a student. I am AWOL from a U.S. Army boot-camp. I couldn't hack the strict drills."

I thought I was having a stroke. I was furious. I was not a U.S. citizen at that time and could have been deported back to Germany for harboring and aiding a deserter to a foreign country. My girls are U.S. citizens. I would have never been able to come back to the U.S. or Canada and possibly would have never seen my girls again. I thanked God that those guards never checked him out. They always checked out everyone during every other trip that was taken to Canada with friends. It was a miracle that this one time, they didn't. He hadn't eaten anything in two days. I gave him a few dollars to get something to eat. After that, I never picked up another hitchhiker again.

While I drove toward the campground, I heard something on the radio about a hurricane warning. I had no idea what a hurricane was. Back in those days, I always carried a small German-English dictionary with me. When I looked up the term "hurricane," it translated to "strong winds." Well, that is no big deal, right? As I drove toward the campgrounds, I did notice something peculiar. Everyone was going in the opposite direction at high speed. I thought it was strange but didn't give it much thought. I just figured that they were all in a hurry to get home early to get a good night's rest before returning back to work the next day.

When I arrived, there was not a single tent or camping trailer in sight. Great. I could pick any lot I wanted. I parked, unlocked the trunk, and got the tent out. I never inspected what my girlfriend gave me. The first thing that was missing were the stakes to secure the tent to the ground. I asked the girls to find some sticks so we could use them. We could put them in at an angle so the loops wouldn't slip out. Then, of course, I needed something to hold the tent up. I looked around for a pole to put in the middle of the tent. I couldn't find one. I did, however, find a piece of rope. There was a loop on top of the tent, so I held the rope between my teeth and climbed up a nearby tree. One of the branches was right over the tent. It looked like it could hold 115 pounds. I crouched onto the branch and slowly inched forward on my stomach, rope dangling from my mouth. I asked my older daughter to grab the loop on top of the tent and hold it up so I could reach it and pull the rope through the loop and secure it around the branch. That should work, right?

Wrong! The next thing I heard was a crash. The branch broke off, and I fell into the tent, toward the ground, still hugging that branch. The tent folded up around me while my girls were trying to find me underneath it all. I couldn't speak for a few seconds. I had the wind knocked out of me!

When they finally uncovered me, I had my eyes closed and wasn't moving. They thought I was dead and they almost became hysterical. I was not hurt. Something softened the blow of my fall. My guardian angel was there. A miracle? The girls were only like nine and thirteen years old. They couldn't drive, and cellphones had not been around at that time. What would they have done? The place was deserted. We finally got it done. A second branch turned out to be stronger.

I returned to the trunk to retrieve the little camping stove. Oops! My friend forgot to include the fuel. No can of Sterno? Okay...so we collected little sticks to start a fire. A man came running out of a small building and said, "Lady, if you want to buy some firewood, then hurry up. I am leaving in two minutes." So I bought one bundle and got a fire started. I had brought homemade spaghetti sauce and pre-boiled spaghetti and meatballs in a cooler. I put everything in a large frying pan to heat it all up. Just because we were camping didn't mean we couldn't enjoy a home-cooked meal, right? Wrong. That was not to be either! It started to rain, dousing out the fire. The sauce was watered down, the spaghetti turned to gel, and the meatballs sort of swam away. The whole mixture overflowed onto the ground.

Still not deterred, I saw another building that looked like a small diner. Hip hip hurray! That'll save the day. Ah—not so fast. The building was locked up tighter than a drum. And what was the name of the little place? The "End of the World Café." How appropriate. Smile.

But, never fear, this mom came prepared. I had also brought some bread, cold cuts, apples, bananas, oranges, celery, and carrot sticks. By then, the wind had picked up and it started to pour. It was cold. We decided the only thing that was left to do was to go to sleep early. So we got our air mattresses, pumped them up, crawled into our sleeping bags fully dressed, and went to sleep, oblivious to the weather outside.

Sometime during the night, I woke up. I was shivering cold and wet. The water in the tent was ankle-deep. We were floating on our air mattresses. Luckily, I had not brought our little suitcases into the tent. They were still in the trunk of the car. We changed into dry clothing and slept the rest of the night in the car. The girls slept in the back and I slept in the front. Back then, the old cars still had bench seats, not bucket seats.

During the night, the wind howled, and several times, it was so strong that one side of the car was lifted up. I was afraid it might turn over. Prayer was the only thing I knew would keep us safe.

In the morning, we got up and saw a little building that said, "Restrooms & Laundry Mat." I hadn't thought of bringing a small camping commode, and I certainly hadn't thought of soaking wet sleeping bags and clothing. I had thought of bringing Canadian money though. I washed everything and put it in the dryer. The girls were cold and sat on top of the dryer to keep warm. The girls were hungry. They wanted breakfast. That presented another dilemma. The only other thing I had brought with me were Lipton's "Cups of Noodle-soup." Okay! That required hot water. Well, this mom was resourceful. All I had to do was put some money in to get a shower and hold the cups under it. Smile. It was hot water.

The campground had also advertised swimming and a beach. All we had to do was to "find it." The only thing we saw was something like a creek or small river. The riverbanks were red clay. It was too cold anyway.

Not a single soul had returned, so we packed everything up and left. On the way out of the campground, both girls begged me, "Please, please never take us camping again." I didn't. Once was enough. As we were leaving, I noticed uprooted trees lying on the ground. By the grace of God, the worst didn't hit the campground but went just around it. Coincidence? Nah. God and angels were with us. It wasn't my time yet. God had a plan for me. I am a work in progress. God isn't finished with me yet.

So we went to Halifax, back to civilization, found a motel with an indoor swimming pool, and "camped out" there. I don't remember what we did the rest of the week—sightseeing or anything. Only the next scary part.

All good things come to an end. It was time to go home. I always worked the graveyard shift—11:00 p.m. to 7:00 a.m.—so the natural thing to do for me is to drive all night because I am awake. Plus, the girls would be asleep and not constantly asking, "are we home yet," ask for a restroom stop, or gripe that they are hungry. I must have chosen a backroad on my way home. All I remember was one long, narrow road making it through nothing but the woods. I felt I was back in Germany, driving through the Black Forest. No streetlights, no homes—absolutely nothing. The only things I encountered were two trucks loaded up with logs. Once or twice, I passed a small sign that said "truckstop." All trucks turn right to be weighed and a small shed beside it. Other than that, nothing. It was a good thing I had a full tank of gas.

At around 6:00 a.m., I saw a McDonald's. An Egg McMuffin sounded good right about then. It was dark and there was no sign of life, so I just drove through. All of a sudden, floodlights came on and a siren started to go off. I looked in the rear-view mirror. What I saw stopped me dead in my tracks. I slammed on the breaks, staying completely still. I didn't know what to do. Next to the little shack stood a uniformed Canadian Border Control officer, holding a rifle at shoulder height, telescope attached, and aimed at my car. I put the car in reverse and drove very slowly back to the shack. He never lowered the gun and kept his finger on the trigger. I prayed, "Dear God, please don't let him shoot me. If he has to shoot, please, please just let him blow out my tires." I finally came back to where he was standing and rolled down my window.

"Why didn't you stop?"

"I thought it was a truck-weighing station."

"Can I see your ID, please?" I showed him my driver's license.

"Where do you live?" I told him where.

"Do you work?"

"Yes."

"Where?"

"GM Syracuse."

"What's the phone number?" I told him.

"Who do I speak to?" I told him.

"Don't move. I am going inside to check out your information." Okay. I wasn't about to take off. I didn't want that Egg McMuffin *that* bad to get shot over it.

He came back and said, "There was no answer when I tried to call."

I answered, "Well, the personnel director for the salaried employees doesn't get to the office until 8:00 a.m." Silently, I prayed: *Please, don't let him call in sick or be on vacation.*

The officer started to interrogate me further. His stone face scared me to death. "What were you doing in Canada?"

"I was vacationing."

"Where were you?"

"End of the World Café."

"Where are you going now?"

"Home."

"Open the trunk." I did. He opened my cooler, cut up my old and stale meatballs, dumped out everything, half-melted ice cubes, opened our luggage, and dumped everything onto the asphalt. He took the trunk apart, and I mean apart. The Cadillac Eldorado had a felt-lined trunk. He ripped it out, checked the spare tire, tire walls, etc. Everything was on the ground at this point.

I dared to ask him, "Who is going to put all of this mess back?"

"You are." Then, he shined his flashlight into the backseat. I don't think that he realized there were two children sleeping in the backseat until then. "Whose kids are these?"

"Mine."

"Wake them up." I did. He asked both of the girls, "Is this your mother?"

They both said, "Yes," and went back to sleep.

By now, it was 8:00 a.m. I picked up the mess minus the meatballs and ice cubes. He went back inside to call GM in Syracuse. When he came out, he said, "Everything checks out. You may leave now." Well gee, thanks. He asked, "If you had nothing to hide, why didn't you stop?" I explained to him that I had expected a big, at least four-lane tollbooth with Canadian Control on one side and American on the other. How was I supposed to know that this little station, no bigger than an "outhouse" built for two, was a checkpoint? Smile. I asked him why he treated me like a criminal. "Well, it is very seldom and unusual for a woman to come alone to this isolated checkpoint." I assumed he was looking for drugs and guns, but kidnapping? I couldn't get away fast enough. I was grateful to be alive. It wasn't my time yet.

I finally got my Egg McMuffin. It had never tasted this good, nor has one since. Thank God that man wasn't trigger-happy.

1979

On December 19 to 20, 2017, early in the morning, I was still half asleep, trying to wake up, when a black and white photo came to mind. An airplane tail was sticking out over a bridge. At first, I was groggy and I wanted to go back to sleep. But slowly, it came back to me. In 1979, a DC 10 had crashed in Washington DC in April or so in 1979, into ice-cold water, and I believe some people died. It had nothing to do with me, so why suddenly did I remember it? My grandmother's (Oma's) 100th birthday! I had three tickets to go to Germany with my two oldest daughters, Patricia, fourteen, and Carla, ten. Today, I was supposed to go to New York City and catch a flight to Frankfurt, Germany.

I received a phone call from the airlines. They told me they didn't have any seats for me on any airplane. All DC 10's had been grounded. They told me, "We're backed up in every airport in the world. Just sit tight, we have you on standby, okay?" The suitcases had already been in the trunk of my car. At about 4:00 AM, I had another call. They said, "We have one seat available if you can have one person in Montreal in two hours." How? We lived in Syracuse, no seats available to Montreal. Am I to send off a ten-year-old by herself into that chaos? Are you kidding me? So I waited and waited. Two days later, I had another phone call. "Can you be in Boston in six hours? We have two seats available." GPS's were not invented at that time. It was 2:00 a.m., no time to call AAA for a road map. Thanks, but no thanks! Finally, on the third day I had the phone call I had been waiting for. Three seats were available from Syracuse to La Guardia and three seats from Kennedy to Stuttgart, Germany. Off we went.

After landing in La Guardia, we took a taxi to Kennedy Airport, checked in our luggage at 6:00 p.m., sat down and waited and waited and waited. By 10:00 p.m., I asked someone at the counter, "Boarding time was at 8:00 p.m., and it is now 10:00 p.m. and we're still waiting. What is the holdup?"

She replied, "Well, we're still transporting the baggage to the plane."

I told her, "Look, I am not blind. I saw the baggage being loaded up between 7:00 and 8:00 p.m. What is really going on?"

"Um, um…you have to wait, okay."

So I sat down and waited. 12:00 a.m. rolled around. Four hundred people are still sitting, lying on luggage, sleeping and waiting.

I finally went back to the counter and said, "Look, why aren't we even boarding yet?"

She said, "Let me make a phone call," and then said, "Well, you may board in a few minutes." And we did.

Again we sat, took naps, and waited again and waited. By 4:00 a.m., I asked the stewardess "What on earth is the problem now? It's 4:00 a.m."

Her answer was, "We are still waiting for the food carts to be delivered."

I told her, "No! I've seen that hours ago. You're lying. I want to know right now what is really going on here?" I could hear noises down below like someone is hitting pipes with a wrench or a hammer. "Don't lie to me again."

She whispered, "We're having engine problems, but we don't want the passengers to know and panic. Look, they're all asleep except for you."

I looked around, true enough. But duh! When they wake up, they expect to be in Germany! Not NYC! "Hello," I said. "Well, but isn't that just grand?" I said, "Now you open up that door and let me out!" She said she couldn't because it was vacuum sealed. I think they'll know the difference. I had spoken with one family from Germany who had five children. They had been on the road, so to speak, for eight days, hopping from one airport to another from LA, commuter planes, or wherever they had seven seats available.

By 6:00 a.m., my daughter Carla woke up and asked. "Are we in Germany yet?"

I said, "No, go back to sleep."

Well, finally I heard the engine rumble, then die, rumble again, and then die again. Finally, we were turning around on the runway, and then nothing. I grabbed the poor stewardess again and asked her again what was wrong. Before she could open her mouth, I said, "And don't you *dare* lie to me again!"

She whispered, "Shh, the generator died."

I said, "Well, now isn't that just *grand*? Now, you open up that door and let me out!"

She said she couldn't because it was vacuum sealed.

I yelled, "Go get the pilot to open that door."

She refused. She said we were at the end of the runway and the ladder has been rolled away. I told her I'd rather jump and break a leg than crash into the ocean and die. At that time, I think I would have preferred to be on a slow boat to China than be on that plane. I finally had to sit back down. The other passengers finally woke up one by one. They all started to chant, "We want to go home, we want to go home, we want to go home." I told them what had happened while they were sleeping, but still they insisted, "We want to go home."

I yelled, "Don't you morons realize you probably won't get there. This old fossil isn't going to make it and we'll all die!" I yelled at the crew, "If we crash in the ocean and die, I'll sue the airlines!" I was so hysterical that I didn't even know how ridiculous that was at the time. There were a few more rumbles, and off we went. Now you would've thought they would taxi the plane around first for a trial run, but oh no, we were at the end of the runway and went straight up. I held my breath and prayed. That was all I could do. Please, God, let us get to Frankfurt safely, save the kids. I'll get off and take a bus or train to my hometown, Schabwisch Gmund.

I took a nap. I woke up someplace around London. I couldn't fall back to sleep, so I just stared out at the clouds. It started to get a little light out. I thought, *Oh good, just a little while longer and we'll be in Frankfurt on the ground and have the wheels beneath us.* I gave a sigh of relief. Great, we've made it. Or did we? The worst was yet to come. Another nightmare unfolded right in front of my eyes. This was just one trip from hell! As I looked out the window and it got light out, I noticed that the wing on the plane was pitch-black, like soot from a fire. I thought, *Now what is going on?* I saw flames underneath the wings leaping up from one of the engines. The plane started to wobble some but then steadied again. I started praying again. "Dear God, please send an army of angels that can carry that plane with their wings to Frankfurt. There are many children on this plane. If it is just *my time*, don't take all the other people with me." I did notice that we were starting to fly a little lower over some towns than usual. I think the pilot was looking for a large open field where we could make an emergency landing in case he would lose another engine. We landed, and I had never been so relieved to be on solid ground. My children had missed the whole drama I went through. There was no point in telling them afterward.

We got to my oma's and mother's condo. Originally, I had planned to be there for ten days. Now, I was already three days late. The airline called my mother's house and asked if I wanted to go home two days earlier. But I had to take a bus to Paris, compliments of the airline, and they would fly us from Paris to Montreal, and then they said I had to find my own way home. Well, I drove from Germany to Paris before and I said, "No thank you!" Firstly, I wanted to stay longer, and secondly, sixty-five years ago, the roads in France still had potholes from World War II, plus the buses didn't have hydraulic suspensions. It is a hard riding trip. I was shocked to realize that they still had problems with catching up to get everyone to their final destinations. But like they say, "It's not over, till the fat lady sings." My short version is, "It's not over 'til it's over." We finally got three seats to go home from Stuttgart, which is forty minutes from my hometown, to Frankfurt to New York City. I should've known better that is not exactly what happened. Well, we did get on a plane in Stuttgart, but did we go to Frankfurt? Oh no! Without telling us, someone decided to make a little detour. Where? Oh, just around the corner to Lisbon, Portugal. We were told we would have a flight out of there to New York City, but the flight to Syracuse, no one knew when. Okay, so we were informed of our flight number, and it was a plane from Argentina. So we sit and wait, sleep on our luggage and wait, go pee and wait, and wait. No such flight number was announced. Planes from all over the world came except from Argentina.

The next morning, someone told us we would get a free breakfast, compliments from the airlines. So we sat at a table, waited, waited, and sure enough, someone brought us a *what?* Are you for *real?* A carafe of red wine with unlimited refills. Sorry for the inconvenience. At 8:00 a.m.? For a ten-year-old and a fourteen-year old? And some Kaiser rolls. I asked for some orange juice, coffee or tea, water, milk; they had nothing. Tap water was not drinkable there sixty years ago. Well, we went back to the gates, waiting. I asked a security guard where our plane from Argentina was. He said it hadn't left Argentina yet. I said, "Why?"

He said, "Well, they have a problem. They have to check it out and see if it's still operational. It hasn't been airborne in fifteen years. It was retired in a junkyard for planes."

Well, I thought, *now* I've heard everything? But had I *seen* everything? Not yet!!!

Well, I finally heard a little excitement from our sorry-looking group. Bedraggled, clothes wrinkled, hair sticking out all over, BO, the whole nine yards. A plane is circling around the air tower, waiting for permission to land.

It was a large bird, no airline logo, no paint job. It looked like a large silver bird in the air. In plain English, metal sheets riveted together, some parts flapping loose. We were assured the parts would be riveted back on. No passengers departed, only crew members. My heart sank when I laid eyes on that contraption. It looked like an old WWII bomber, like a parachute plane, etc.; everything but a passenger plane. But rest assured, it had been converted before retirement. I would have had more confidence in a flying lawnmower than this relic. We had no choice; we had to take a chance. It was practically on its maiden voyage for a transatlantic flight. This was it, the try-out. That made me feel so much better. When we took off, all I could do was say a prayer. "Heavenly Father, Lord Jesus, Holy Spirit, Mother of God, and all the angels, please hold these rivets together. Don't let it fall apart. A little spit and chewing gum would also help. Amen!"

The plane sort of creaked and made noises, but everything seemed fine until the captain announced that we were running low on fuel and we had to make an emergency landing. We did, but it was in the middle of nowhere in the woods, someplace in Newfoundland. No airport, no population, no town, no nothing. So again, we waited and waited. We were informed that the Royal Air Force is sending a tanker full of fuel and breakfast for everyone. Ah, it just couldn't get better than that! I think a trip with the motorcycle gang, Hell on Wheels, probably would have been more enjoyable. If that vacation, if you can call it that, wasn't miraculous, I don't know what is.

My oma died in 1980. I always joked with her, "Oma, you can't die until I see you one more time." God, made it possible. That is all she wanted—to see me and the girls. It wasn't my time yet. I don't know who was happier when we finally made it home, our guardian angels or me? We landed at JKF and took a taxi to La Guardia just as the airport closed down. We had to spend another night in the airport and caught an early flight to Syracuse. That is when my life was spared again.

Husband #3

In case someone doesn't believe in spirits, they are real. Five or six years later, I remarried for the third time. What was I thinking? In January 1980, my bed shook violently. Gary—six-foot-four, two hundred pounds—and I both bolted up from a deep sleep about 2:00 a.m. He looked dazed and said, "What was that?"

I pushed him back down and said, "Go back to sleep!" I had heard my grandmother calling my endearment name, only she used Brigittle. My name is Brigitte, but in the German language, sometimes instead of saying "little" or "small" in front, you add "le" or "chen" at the end. For example, the word for child is 'kind." Instead of saying a "small child," you would say *kindchen* or *kindle*. The next morning, we watched the news, read the weather report in the paper, asked my neighbors if they felt a small rumbling from an earthquake. There was nothing. I knew my oma died and said goodbye.

When my two daughters from my first marriage were ages ten and fourteen, I had "empty nest" syndrome. I had one miscarriage after another. With husband number three, I was home just sitting down for supper, when all of a sudden, I felt a pain. I ran to the bathroom, sat on the toilet, and I heard a big splash. I had had a miscarriage. I let out a scream! My husband and my two daughters came running. Blood was gushing out of me. I lay on the floor. The blood sprayed out of me. The placenta was up front. My husband told me later he had to clean up the floor and walls up to six feet. I instructed my husband to call my doctor and told my daughter to go next door and call an ambulance. I was in the ambulance at least twenty to thirty minutes in front of my house. Why we were just sitting there instead of going to the hospital? They said they were waiting here because they're calling to see which hospital could take me. I lived in Minoa, New York, probably fifteen minutes away from the closest hospital and twenty minutes from the furthest on Onondaga Hill. So I said, "Go down 690 to the underpass and wait there." St Joseph's was to the right, two to three minutes away, Upstate Medical also two to three minutes away to the left, and Onondaga Hill was maybe a few miles straight ahead; it would save us at least thirty minutes later on when they got the call. While we waited under the overpass, they got the call; St Joe's can take me. Dr. Waldman was waiting for me.

By then, I started to get lightheaded from the loss of blood. I was laying on the gurney in the hallway. I started to fade away. It was around 8:00 p.m. They elevated my legs and covered me with blankets to keep me warm. I was freezing, had the chills, etc. At midnight, my doctor came to me and said, "Brigitte, I don't know what to do. I have called all blood banks in three counties. They supply thirty-five hospitals, but you have something extra in your blood, and no one knows what to give you. If you have a reaction, you'll die."

I said, "Well, I've lost five pints of blood, and I'm going to die a hundred percent. If you give me something, I have a 50-50 chance to make it."

So he said, "I can try liquid protein or plasma. I just don't know which. I am undecided." He was clearly distressed. I was only thirty-six years old. Up to that point, he said he had never lost a patient.

So I told him, "Just give me what you think is best, and if I don't make it, please don't feel bad. You did your best." I told him that I'm tough like my oma and she lived to be 101 years old, survived two World Wars, buried a husband and a daughter, and I refused to die before 101.

After that, I lost consciousness, I never knew what he gave me. Years later, I found out I had an extra enzyme in my blood which is supposed to be common in European aristocrats. One of my ancestors was a baron. Like many lower-level noblemen, they dropped their titles before and after the wars. When I came to, he smiled and said, "It's like a miracle!"

I still had the "empty nest" syndrome, so I kept trying. The next disaster came a year later. I was pregnant again, and my doctor put me on bed rest. I stopped working, but with a husband and two teenagers to chauffeur around, shopping, cooking, cleaning, etc., that wasn't entirely possible. Animal tendons had been sewn on the top of my cervix to hold it together and prevent the cervix from dilating. My two oldest girls were two and three months early. I took it as easy as I could. One night, husband number three and I were watching TV. After the news around 11:30 p.m., he turned off the TV and said, "Let's go to bed."

I felt a heavy pressure and said, "Go ahead, I'll be there in a while."

He was a control freak and insisted that I get up "right now!"

I said, "No, just let me lay here a little longer."

His answer, "No wife of mine is a pig and a slob and sleeps fully dressed in the living room on a recliner." He roughly yanked me out of the chair, and my water broke.

He did take me to a hospital. It wasn't a Catholic hospital. The doctor said he wants to do a C-section. The control-freak monster said, "No, I don't want my wife to have a zipper," meaning a scar. Now, I needed my husband's consent to have a C-section. I begged and pleaded with him, but like always, if I said yes to anything, he would say no. It was a power play.

The doctor couldn't do anything, so he said, "We'll keep her here to put extra weight on the baby." My daughter, Carla, was born at twenty-four weeks, the same time as this little boy. After two weeks, the doctor said again, "I advise to do a C-section."

Again the same answer, "I don't want my wife to have a zipper—no." And he left.

The next morning, around 10:00 a.m. I felt a chill. The hair on my arms were standing up. There was no open window or a draft coming from anywhere. I called a nurse. She brought a fetal monitor; everything seemed fine. They took blood samples. The normal white blood cell count is 30,000; mine was 70,000. I asked for my doctor (not Dr. Walderman at the time). They said he went on vacation. Three resident doctors came in and out, checking the monitor. The heartbeat of the baby became irregular and sometimes stopped when the baby moved. The doctors reached inside, turned the baby, and the heartbeat resumed. I begged for a C-section; they wouldn't do it. I had a telephone on my nightstand. I asked the nurse to bring me a phone book. She did, but before she handed it to me, she said, "What do you need it for?" I told her the truth. I said I wanted to call my attorney. I wanted him to see a judge and get a court order to perform a C-section. She took the phone book and the phone away from me and walked away.

In the meantime, the baby's heartbeat continued to be irregular, stop and go, etc. By then, I had a high fever. The three resident doctors then decided to do an emergency C-section. By the time I was wheeled into the operating room, the baby had died, and my temperature was dangerously high. They put three different antibiotics in the IV, but the fever didn't break. I was put on a rubber mattress. A nurse put a bucket of ice cubes by my feet and emptied out lukewarm water by my head. She worked tirelessly for the whole eight hour shift. Then she said, "Lift up your gown. I'll wrap ice cubes in a towel and put it on your chest."

I didn't feel the ice cubes; they just melted. Then she came back with a bucket of ice cubes and said, "It'll be cold, but I am going to put them directly on your chest." I didn't feel anything except hot water dripping on the sheet and a sizzling sound when the ice cubes came in contact with my skin. Two nurses came and took my temperature under my arm the thermometer exploded.

Now, another doctor came in and said, "We have tried everything. You will not see the sun come up. I have been here for thirty-six hours, delivered ten babies, and I have to get some sleep. There is nothing I can do for you." The next morning, she was surprised I hadn't died. Another miracle?

I was thirty-nine years old, and everybody looked at me with pity and sad eyes. She asked me if I wanted someone to call my husband. I said no, but three doctors and three nurses called him all night long. They all received the same answer, "No, I am not coming. I need my beauty rest. I have to work in the morning. If she makes it I'll see her in the morning. If she doesn't, there's nothing I can do." And he went back to sleep. After that, I resigned myself to the fact that I'm going to die.

I had a warm peaceful feeling and I thought, *Well, if this is how it feels to die, it is a nice feeling.* I closed my eyes and thought, *My oldest daughter, Patty, is fourteen. She is strong-willed. She knows what she wants. She'll be all right.* Then, as I thought of my second daughter, I thought, *Oh my God, she is only ten. She still needs her mother.* I felt like a bolt of lightning went through my whole body, and I felt like someone branded her name in my brain, *Carla.* At that instant, the fever broke. I had called God's name, and a miracle occurred.

Prince Charming showed up about 6:00 a.m. I started crying and said, "The baby died!"

His reply was "So what, the sucker died. Have another one." I hated him with every fiber of my heart. I always blamed him for the baby's death. If he hadn't yanked me out of the recliner and later gave his permission for a C-section, the baby would be a thirty-six-year-old young man. I also blamed myself for not walking out of that hospital and going to St Joseph's, a Catholic hospital. They would have done a C-section. We believe to save the baby first and the mother second. I told him to let them take the baby and not worry about me, I said, "I'm tough, I'll make it. I'm going to be 101 years old like my grandmother." I always had that feeling, even today.

His only response was "What am I going to do with the baby by myself?"

I cannot understand why I needed his consent. I am carrying the baby and I have nothing to say in the matter? After I came home three days later, I asked my husband if he's made funeral arrangements. He said, "No, I had him cremated, it's cheaper." When I asked where the urn and the ashes were, his answer was, "I didn't pick him up." Again, it was done without anyone consulting the mother. Why?

I still had the "empty nest" syndrome. After one or two more miscarriages, I finally had a healthy little girl. Soon after that, I kicked my husband to the curb. He was my sperm bank, he'd outlived his purpose, and that was that. The honeymoon was over. He wouldn't move out at first; his attorney told him that he could stay in his marital home until the day the divorce was final. Well, this little woman finally asserted herself. I bought a four-bedroom Colonial two houses up the street. I made more money than he did. I didn't say a word. I waited until he went to Canada on a fishing trip with his dad. I packed all his personal belongings in cardboard boxes and dropped them off at "Mamsie's," his nickname for his mother. She took them silently, no questions asked. She knew about his cheating, threats to kill me, etc.

He was seventeen when he went to Vietnam and the army taught him to kill. He couldn't understand why he couldn't kill anymore. He said he thoroughly enjoyed it. He enjoyed hanging "gooks," Viet Cong, to slit their throats from one ear to the other, or sneaking up behind them and breaking their necks, etc. He said he had the "killer instinct" and he still does a job occasionally for the government, the CIA, if they wanted to eliminate someone. One day, I had enough and I said, "Go ahead, I'd rather be dead than live with you."

Then he changed his tune, "Okay, no, I am going to let you live, kill the kids, and make you watch."

I said, "Your daughter is only eighteen months old."

He said, "She's lived a lot longer than other kids."

I said, "Like who?"

I guess when civilians in Vietnam, mostly women and children were rescued by helicopter and there was only room for one more, some women killed their babies and took their pigs on board. They could always have another child but couldn't afford to buy another pig. Well, since I probably had enough money to buy a small pig farm and didn't much care for little piggies, I chose to keep my kids, thank you very much!

Another Divine Intervention

In January 1981, another miracle occurred. It's the only explanation I can think of. I usually worked from 11:00 p.m. to 7:00 a.m. That night, I was home. Friday night was our Saturday, and I had the weekend off. I had just met Gary Macko at a Christmas party. That night, both of my older daughters, Patricia and Carla, were spending the night at their friend's house. In the basement, I had a couch, TV, and an old kitchen table with chairs where the girls usually sat to do their homework or play board games. In front of the table, there was a large furnace. It looked like it had been an old wood or coal furnace converted to gas. A few days earlier, I had noticed that the furnace wouldn't shut off. I had to shut it off manually. It had reached over 90 degrees. That evening, Gary had come over. We watched TV then had a pizza sitting by the table. When we were done, he left, and I went to bed. During the night, I was jolted awake. There was a large *boom,* and the house shook a little. It sounded like an explosion down in the basement. I got up and went downstairs. What I saw shook me up. I obviously forgot to turn off the furnace because it had exploded. Its heavy cast-iron door had blown off and flew over the table and was leaning against the basement wall. A few hours earlier, we were sitting at that table. That door would have killed us both. For weeks, I had nightmares, visualizing either me or my daughters sitting there, getting killed. I don't think it was just luck. God and our guardian angels were protecting us. It wasn't our time yet.

What is strange is that I had forgotten all about it. Just as I had thought I remembered everything and my booklet was finished, this popped into my mind. It's like God saying, "Hey, you forgot to give me praise or credit for one more incident where I was with you." That was February of 2018. I have a tendency to forget everything unpleasant but...your subconscious buries or stores everything only to surface sooner or later at the right moment. When you praise the Lord, do it right and give him the glory for everything. Don't leave anything out.

P.S. Your "subconscious mind" is like a thought transfer. It picks up vibrations much like radio waves. So God had to be present to give me that thought. God gave me a gentle nudge to remember.

Fireworks of a Different Kind

1990

It was about 9:30 p.m., just starting to get dark as I was sitting in my backyard, enjoying the peace and quiet, when I heard a few fireworks go off in the neighborhood. I wasn't thinking about anything in particular, when all of a sudden, the words "crackling and sparkles" came to mind. I didn't think it was unusual; after all, fireworks were going off around me. At around 10:00 p.m., I took another quick dip in the pool to cool off before going inside. As I drifted around lazily on my noodle, looking up to see if any stars were out, my eyes fixed on the utility pole in the front yard. That is when I remembered another house, another pool, and another pole.

It was back in Minoa, New York, around maybe 1990. It was in the afternoon. The girls were taking a nap, so I thought, *I'll enjoy swimming by myself for a change, no splashing, I won't have to go down the slide with my youngest, no music blaring, no yelling "Don't run!,"* etc. It was heavenly. The silence was deafening. Smile. That is when I heard a crackling sound. I looked around, but I didn't see anything that could have made this kind of sound. Behind our yard was a cemetery, and there was no funeral being held on the other side of the fence, nothing. I had also heard it the previous day but shrugged it off. I was floating on my back, looking up, when I saw sparks up by the utility pole. The top of the pole was black, charred from the sparks from exposed wires. Oh my god, the village homes were close together, more long than wide. If these sparks had burned away more of the wood, those live wires would have swung right down between the houses, into the pool, and electrocuted whoever was in the water, mostly children and myself.

I ran into the house, called the village office to send someone ASAP. I kept the children inside, of course. I was shook up. Those electric sparks had been flying at least for the twenty-four hours that I had heard it. Who knows how long before that? I said a prayer of thanks. It truly was a miracle that the utility pole didn't catch fire and the wire landed in the pool. Now, thinking back, I am wondering how many blessings can one person receive? Are they numbered? Is my quota up? Are they infinite? God has a plan for all of us, and until I fulfill his plan for me, it is not my time.

Demolition Derby

Around 1992

My oldest daughter turned out to be a daredevil. When she was around eighteen, she wanted a car. I told her to go pick one out and I would pay for it—*not*—when I saw it. An old black Mustang. Paint job! What paint job? It looked like someone took a toothbrush and painted it with tar. For some reason, she was never able to register and drive it on the road. The guy who sold it to her "saw her coming;" a young, naïve girl who had her heart set on a Mustang. She did get it going.

In her last year of high school, she took "auto-mechanics." She had enough credits to graduate after three years. The reason she was one year ahead was my fault. I had enrolled her at Bishop Grimes High School. On the first day of school, she came home and said, "Mom, you have to go to school tonight and sign me up for classes." I asked her if she was coming with me. She said no, it is only for parents. Okay…so I went.

There were ten tables set up. I signed her up for everything. Art, German, French, Italian, and Latin amongst them all. When she came home the next day, she seemed angry. Sarcastically, she said, "Thanks a lot, Mom."

I asked her, "For what?"

She said, "For signing me up for everything." She went into her bedroom and slammed the door. I was dumbfounded. Isn't that what I was supposed to do? I never went to school in this country, so I didn't know how "things worked" over here. She asked me if she could "drop" some classes.

I said, "No, quitting is not an option. You'll stick it out for one year, then you can drop what you did not like." Well, any other kid might've "flunked" what they didn't like; but not my Patty. 92 was her lowest mark and 98 was the highest in all of the languages she was taking. She was a good trooper.

So even though she had enough credits to graduate after three years, I wouldn't let her. I wanted her to go another year and finish with her friends. I didn't want her to go to college at seventeen and out into the "adult" work. My oma always said, "You are only a child for a little while and an adult for the rest of your life, full of responsibilities." Truer words had never been spoken. I really didn't know what courses she took that year, except for the one in auto-mechanics.

That eyesore of a Mustang sat in front of the house for several years. She wouldn't part with it. That was her baby! Then one day, she started to rip out the passenger and back seats and all of the rest of the interior. I asked her what in the world she was doing. She replied nonchalantly, "I'm getting my car ready for the "demolition derby" in the state-fair in Syracuse, New York."

"You *what*? Are you out of your mind? You have no experience and are going to get yourself killed!"

I couldn't talk her out of it. When the day arrived, I went to watch her. About thirty cars or so were lined up. Each driver had to stand next to the car before they started. Of course, my daughter was the only "girl." She bumped several cars and disabled them, skillfully avoiding getting hit by other cars. Soon into the race, only two cars were left. You might've guessed…one of them was my daughter. Now, not only do you have to stay away from one car, you also have to slalom around the other twenty-eight cars. No big deal for my daughter. I mean, after all, who taught her to drive? Mom! In the old country when I learned how to drive, at that time at least, you "weaved" in and out of traffic fast. My girls always called me lead-foot. I wondered why. I guess everybody was in a hurry to be first at the stop sign. Then you could be first to gun ahead of the traffic. There is no speed limit on the Autobahn in Germany. Surprisingly, fewer accidents take place there than over here.

Well…then the unexpected happened. A tire blew on the Mustang and disabled her car. The other guy won. I figured that would be the end of it. But, oh no, quitting was not an option. Next September, she enrolled herself again into the derby. This time it got a little "hairy."

On the day of the demolition derby, I went to the state fair. My girlfriend, Ute, and her husband, Werner, were on vacation from Germany and were there with us. So of course, I wanted them to see the event. When the designated time came, we sat on the bleachers. They, of course, found it astonishing that my daughter, a girl, participated.

Well, at the start, everything went fine. Halfway through, her car stopped. Flames were shooting out from underneath the car. "Oh my god, please don't let that gas-tank explode… Not my Patty. Not my Patty!" It was a rule that no one was allowed to get out of a disabled vehicle, or that person will get run over by other cars. I ran down from the bleachers, screaming, "Patty, Patty, fire, fire, get out, get out!" On the bottom of the bleachers was what looked like a twenty-foot-high chain-link fence with barbed-wire on top. My daughter sat still, not moving her head to the left or the right. She just looked straight ahead. I screamed, I yelled, I even did jumping jacks all to get her attention. Nothing worked. I became hysterically terrified. I had already seen her blown up to bits and pieces in my mind.

I took my shoes off, trying to get my toes in the chain-links and climb that fence. Werner pulled me down. I was too petrified to even cry. Unless someone actually saw a child—no matter what the age—killed in front of their eyes, then they would not be able to imagine the emotional anguish I felt. I was in total shock. Finally, a fire engine came. What a sight that was. It was small. It looked like it came out of a museum; the first fire engine ever built. I am not sure if it had one of those handles you have to crank to get it started. I didn't pay attention to any of the small details other than the fact that it was small and slow. All I could do was look horrified and pray, "Dear God, please let them get to her in time. Please, please!!" I felt like pushing that piece of metal. I think it was a miracle.

When I told a few guys about it, they laughed at me and said, "Gas tanks don't explode in real life—that only happens in the movies." Well, last week, April 19, 2018, I watched the national news. An SUV crashed into a house. The car exploded and went up in flames. So did the house. It collapsed. Three people were rescued from the house. Tell that to these people that it only happens in the movies. God heard my pleas.

After all of this happened, Patty joined the Marines. Her daredevil days came to a stop for a while, but then the next thing I knew, I was receiving videos from Okinawa, Japan: cliff diving, bungee jumping, hang gliding from California, snorkeling in Hawaii, parachuting, and, oh yeah, let's not forget taking race car driving lessons somewhere in the world (I can't remember where). She kept her guardian angels busy.

She retired from the Marines after serving twenty-two years. She now has two little boys. I can hardly wait to see what they are going to do some day to upstage Mommy dearest. I pray for them also. They are going to need it!

Mopsy Dies and Saves Lives!

1992

It was a beautiful, sunny, cloudless day; the hottest since 1962. I was floating on a noodle in my pool when the phone rang. I had put a small side table next to the ladder. My daughter, Jennifer, had left at 5:30 a.m. to go camping someplace in Pennsylvania. Now did she call to ask how I was? Oh no! Her biggest concern was Zoe, her little mutt, a mixture of a pug and a Chihuahua. She said she doesn't want to come home to find that Zoe had met the same demise as Flopsy. Huh? Flopsy? What and who was Flopsy?

She had to repeat the name Flopsy at least four to five times before it rang a bell. Ah, now I got it. I hear you loud and clear. Flopsy was a rabbit we had twenty-five years ago. Flopsy was named after his long floppy ears, I suppose. Now, mind you, he wasn't a cute little white Easter Bunny; he was a big, fat, black, twenty-five-pound monster and dumb as a rock. All he ever did was sit and twitch his nose. I mean, what good was he as a pet? He didn't fetch, jump, roll over, dance, stand up on his hind legs and beg for a bone, nothing, nada. The kids loved him. I had bought a small collar and a leash. The girls took him for a walk, I mean, a hop, down the bunny trail, a.k.a. the sidewalk, followed by all the neighborhood children. All twenty-one of them! School let out by 2:00 p.m., and ten minutes later, they all assembled in front of my house waiting for Flopsy.

I usually kept him in the basement in a huge kennel. It was cooler down there. That fateful afternoon, I brought him up at 1:30 p.m. into the backyard, put on the collar and leash, ready for his outing, only this time, it was to be his funeral. He had suffocated, his fur was too thick, and he was overheated. My youngest daughter, Jennifer, was maybe five or six. She came running back in the house, crying and screaming, "You rabbit killer! You killed my Flopsy!" Oh boy, did you ever hear twenty-one kids crying, wailing, and giving you the evil eye? Jennifer has never forgiven me—for twenty-five years. A few weeks later, I went back to the man who I nicknamed the rabbit farmer. I bought Flopsy's brother for $20. Identical in color and size. If you were a connoisseur of rabbit meat, your mouth would salivate. That pacified the children somewhat, and grudgingly, I had gotten back into their good graces. They named him Mopsy. This time, I left Mopsy in the basement and waited for the girls to bring him up to play with. Well, peace was restored in my little family and neighborhood kids. But—there is always a "but."

Larry, husband number four, started twitching his nose, sniffing, and announcing, "I smell gas. Call the utility company and ask them to send someone to check out the pipes." They did, but they couldn't find any leaks. I have sinus problems and can't smell anything that faint. Larry insisted that he was smelling gas and had me call Niagara Mohawk four more times.

They started to get irritated and said, "We can't find a leak, give it up. We can't just keep on sending our men out there for nothing. Maybe there is a dead mouse in the house and that is what stinks." Oh boy, Larry got on the phone, and after a shouting match, Larry won. They said, "Yes, we will send out someone again." We were treated as a nuisance. I would have given up after the second visit.

Well, that someone came. He and Larry went into the basement. The first thing I heard was, "No, I did not kill that rabbit. We don't eat our pets!" That man found, not only one, but four tiny gas leaks, the size of pinholes! Gas is what killed that rabbit. Now, the moral or miracle of that story is, Larry and I each smoked three packs of cigarettes a day. That is a total of 120 cigarettes. Our Bic lighters flicked over 100 times a day. It was a miracle that we didn't blow ourselves up. If that doesn't convince anyone that there is a higher power looking out for us, I don't know what would. It wasn't just a dead rabbit and Larry's nose that saved us, although Larry's nose came in handy. It was the grace of God, and it wasn't my time yet. I guess you could say Flopsy and Mopsy were the black clouds with a silver lining. I hope they have a special place in the animal kingdom.

Larry's Nose

Yesterday, I had remembered the tragic demise of Flopsy and Mopsy. But now that triggered yet another "near miss" for this little family. The keyword was nose, Larry's sensitive honker. Smile. That also happened around 1990 to 1992. I worked the graveyard shift from 10:30 p.m. to 7:00 a.m. When I came home, my two younger daughters, Heidi and Jennifer, were usually up waiting for me to fix breakfast. After that, I normally went upstairs to go to sleep. During the week, I had a babysitter, Marlene, stay with us from Sunday night until Friday noon. Larry stayed with the girls on weekend mornings, as I usually worked seven nights a week.

One Saturday morning, I had just gone upstairs, starting to doze off when I heard Larry yell, "Fire, fire!" Of course that woke me up. I flew down the stairs, ran through the living room, dining room, kitchen, and then the TV room, where the girls were watching cartoons. I screamed at them to go outside and yelled at Larry, "Call 911!" Then I looked around for flames, but I didn't see anything. The basement was the only place I hadn't checked yet. Larry was running around frantically and, what seemed to me, aimlessly with his arms up in the air. I looked at him and asked, "Larry where is the fire?"

He replied, "I don't know."

I said, "You what? You don't know!"

Again, he said, "No, but I can smell it."

I was thinking, *Are you already drunk by 10:00 a.m.? What is wrong with you! What have you been smoking in your pipe!* I was furious for having been interrupted from my beauty sleep, because I usually only got three hours a day. I went back upstairs and tried to get some more z's. A few minutes later, he yelled again, "Fire, fire!" I ran downstairs again. Nothing! Now I was really disgusted, steam was coming out of my nose. He said, "Listen to me. I can smell electrical wires burning—it must be behind the walls. Help me pat down the walls. I've smelled it many times in large restaurant kitchens."

I thought, *Yeah, right, and I walk on water.* I humored him and did as he said. He started in the kitchen and I went into the TV room. He told me to check especially around all the switches and outlets. So I did. Lo and behold, I found one that felt hot to the touch. He ran down to the basement and switched off all the breaker panels. Then he punched a hole in the wall, and sure enough, the coating around the wires had melted and the wires were touching. It was an old village home, built before electric stoves, TVs, air conditioning, microwaves, refrigerator, fans, etc. I was shocked. God, in his infinite wisdom, gave us a nose with a sense of smell. We were spared again. Thank you, Lord. But that wasn't the last miracle I experienced in that house. God is watching over me 24/7.

I Think God Plays Chess

I was out of work approximately from 1993 to 1998. During that time, I had a cleaning lady named Toots. She came to my house every Wednesday morning. One Wednesday morning though, she called and said she couldn't come. She was in Chittenango, New York, with her grandsons, and she didn't have transportation to come to Minoa, New York, that day. I told her that wouldn't be a problem, I'll come and pick her up and then take her home to Bridgeport, New York.

On the way back, I took the back roads, one stretch along the Erie Canal. At one point, there was a sharp, hairpin curve. Just as I came around the corner, which was a tight, sharp, right-hand turn, two big Bucks, each an eight-pointer, stood in the middle of the road. The road was narrow. To the right was a down-sloping bank into the canal and to the left was an uphill bank. I had no place to go but to plow right into the two deer. There was no time for an "angel whisperer" message from God.

I didn't even put my foot on the brake; there just wasn't enough time or space to stop. I knew the deer would be scooped up, land on the hood, crash through the windshield, and land in the car. Toots and I would be crushed to death. The only thought I had was *God, wait! The kids, not the kids!* They were three and eight. I closed my eyes and waited for the blow. It never came.

I felt something. I opened my eyes, my foot still on the gas pedal, still in drive, yet standing still. I looked back to my right. The deer to my right was just standing down by the canal, looking at us. Then I looked to my left. That deer also stood still, just looking at us. I was in shock. I couldn't move. I was frozen on the spot. Then I made eye contact with the deer on the left. He nodded his head. He was what I would call a majestic animal. And something in my head said, *Go, go with God, just go*. That's when I came to my senses. I looked at Toots.

She had a dazed, unbelieving look in her eyes and said, "What just happened?" I couldn't answer.

Even though she continued cleaning for me for a few more years, we never ever talked about it. I felt like a hand from above had moved the car to the middle of the road and placed each deer, one to the right and one to the left. Just like figures in a chess game. Each figure standing still. Had a "miracle" occurred? You betcha. It wasn't my time yet.

Workman's Compensation

I usually worked the 11:00 p.m. to 7:00 a.m. midnight shift. Then there was a time I was out on worker's compensation. During this time in the evenings, from 9:00 p.m. to 11:00 p.m., I usually relaxed and watched a movie. The girls were in bed, sleeping of course. I would watch the news until 11:30, put some clothes in the washer, sit at the kitchen table, and read. I was a night owl. Every night at midnight sharp, I would see a black shadow come up the basement stairs, sort of hover around the TV room, through the kitchen, dining room, living room, and up the stairs to the bedrooms. I never followed the black cloud upstairs. I wasn't afraid because the shadow never came near me, but it always floated on the opposite wall. Since the shadow or cloud resembled a small, little old lady with a curved back, I immediately thought it was my beloved oma. So for two years, I spoke to that shadow in German, "Oma, I am fine, the girls are fine. Please go on over to the other side and rest in peace." I did that almost every night for two solid years. Every night, the cloud appeared.

Then one afternoon, there was a knock on my door. A young teenage boy stood on the front porch. He said, "Hi, Brigitte, may I come in?" It was Todd, who had been living here when he was four years old.

I said, "Of course." His mother and his siblings had lived here for maybe three or four years. She was a young widow with four small children between the ages of ten down to three years old. Unfortunately, she tipped the wine bottle a little too much. One Christmas Eve at 5:00 p.m. she realized she didn't have a tree yet. One bedroom was stacked from bottom to top with presents but no tree. She put her four children, plus a friend of theirs, in her car. She hit a tree head-on and died instantly. One of her sons was in critical condition. All four children had to go live in California with relatives. A few years earlier, his father had also hit a tree head-on and died instantly. Todd was visiting relatives in the Syracuse area and wanted to visit his old home to see if it had changed. I invited him in to look around.

That's when it hit me! That shadow is not my Oma; it is Pat, a mother looking for her children. That night, I sat at my kitchen table at 11:55 pm, purposely waiting for my "visitor." As the cloud was floating by, I said in

English, "Pat, Todd was here today. He is fine. I asked him how his siblings are doing and he told me all are doing well. Go over to the other side and rest in peace." That was the last time I have seen her. At the time, I thought God meant for me to buy this house. If someone else bought it who was not familiar with the circumstances, they wouldn't be able to send that young woman's soul to rest. Coincidence? I don't think so, because at that time, I had already signed a purchase offer on another four-bedroom home. I was able to break the contract because of a technicality. It had something to do with the windows. The real estate lady for the seller of that house said she had never heard of such a thing. One of the reasons I wanted the house up the street was because my daughter, Carla, didn't want to change schools.

After I had moved into the new house, I was out on workman's compensation. I had transferred to the paint department of General Motors, in Syracuse, to clean the paint booth. I had to take a stainless steel knife, cut up the rubber, one-inch thick paint, and spray paint the booth with fresh paint for the day shift. Sometimes a coworker and I had to go up on the roof and clean the oven. It was a steel housing that covered the whole building. We had to vacuum the walls, ceilings, and floor. It had to be dust free so the dust specks wouldn't settle on the freshly painted cars and bake on the paint. We wore white plastic disposable coveralls, protective suits, over our regular clothing. We had to go upstairs on the outside of the building to a walkway and then into the oven from the outside. The large doors were vacuum-sealed and extremely hard to open. My partner was a six-foot-two man, two-hundred-twenty pounds, and he was able to yank the doors open. Before we would go up, he locked out the heating system. Only two people had keys to it—my partner and the security guards. One night, my partner said, "Brigitte, it is getting awfully hot in here. I'm going downstairs to the locker room, take off my street clothes, and just put my plastic suit on, I'll be right back." He never did. The place got warmer and warmer—downright hot. My gold necklace and my gold bracelet started to burn and leave red marks on my skin. The bottom of my shoes started to melt. I panicked. Someone had turned the oven on to 450 degrees, leaving me to fry to death. I threw my whole weight, shoulders first, against the door. It wouldn't budge. Now, the way the oven works was as follows. First, the unpainted parts were loaded, placed on hooks, and a chain-driven motor moved the parts through to paint booths where robots sprayed the paints. Then a man would also have a paint gun to give it a finishing touch if the robots missed a spot. Then the line would slowly move to a metal duct, going up to the oven on the roof, moving slowly through the baking process. The parts would travel back and forth several times. The whole process would take over two hours. I had no way out.

I panicked and prayed, "Dear God, don't let me die up here, a horrible death."

Something said, *Go down the chute.*

The chutes were small, pitch dark, and had iron hooks hanging from the low ceiling. I couldn't crawl or my hands and knees would have been burned. So I crouched and slowly crept down, using my elbows to feel for hooks so they wouldn't hit my face. I knew someone tried to kill me. I knew just who it was. I never suspected my partner, but he was afraid of the "evil trio." They tried to run me off the road, slit my tires, etc. After that, I noticed a blue Cadillac following me to work, and it was there, by the gate at 7:00 p.m., following me home at a distance. It was John Gotti's car, bought at an auction in New York City by the Syracuse Mafia. My boyfriend, unbeknownst to me, had connections. He was a "bagman" and the guy with the baseball bat breaking kneecaps. He had ordered the "escort" for my protection. They just couldn't kill me, even if they tried, and try they did! I was locked in a smaller oven a second time. Again, my partner excused himself and left. This time though, I didn't wait too long to look for an escape route.

There was only one problem; this oven was used for smaller parts, and hence, the shaft-duct system was a lot smaller. The opening wasn't any larger than the tunnel in an MRI machine. I had to lay down, flat on my back, cross my arms in front of me, and slid down. In front of the chute, there was a bench, and the supervisor, Dick B., held a meeting with all five of us. When he saw me come down, he immediately saw that I was overheated, my face was beet-red, and he told me to go see the nurse. I waved him off and said, "No, I'm fine." He asked me what happened. I just said, "Nothing, I always come down this way." I used to joke and say I'm like a German tank, plowing through everything, only in my case, sliding.

Of course, the "evil trio" was there when I first came down the duct. They smirked. When Dick asked me what happened, they held their breath and looked worried. When I said nothing, they let out a sigh of relief. I smiled at them. I mean, what would have been the point? It was my word against three.

I would have been made out to be a liar and troublemaker. I didn't want them to give them the satisfaction to know I was upset and feared for my life. To them, it was only a prank. Ya think! They kept harassing me anyway they could think of, too numerous to mention.

Then one day, a new supervisor, Tony, a young Italian man, came to the paint department. How that happened, I'll never know. He was from a temp agency, cocky, and a know-it-all. He had no idea what jobs each of us were assigned to or our job task. He just said, "You all know what to do, so go do it." Then he left and slept all night until morning about an hour and a half before the shift ended. He walked up to me one morning and said to go to the storage area and bring over a fifty-five-gallon drum of rip-off paint. That is what we called it. I looked at him and had to carefully phrase my words. If I said, "No," I could be fired on the spot and a guard would come ask me to get my purse, coat, etc., and escort me out the door. I had two daughters in college, one in kindergarten, and one in pre-k. I simply couldn't afford to get fired.

The trio was close by, smirking, waiting, and hoping I would get fired. I cautiously, simply said, "I can't do the job, not that I won't."

He asked, "Why not?"

I said, "Do I look like I can physically do the job?"

He said, "Yes."

Now, I'm 5-foot tall and weighed 110 pounds at that time. I asked him how tall his wife was and the weight of her. It was similar to mine. I asked him, "Would you ask your wife to do it?"

He said yes. He told me that I had done it before and people have seen me. I said name me just one person who saw me. There wasn't except for the three evil ones. I tried to help the guy out and said, "At least give me one person to help me."

He said no. He had an audience and tried to save face. I told him that the past practice was to have a forklift truck deliver it. He answered, "I don't have the luxury of a forklift truck driver on the night shift."

I told him that I know that, but when I was a supervisor in shipping on the eleven to seven shift, the paint room supervisor would call and ask me to have one of my drivers do it. Now, I must have struck a nerve!

"Are you trying to tell me how to do my job?" His audience snickered. Maybe he felt belittled? Humiliated? A little woman telling him what to do?

Or embarrassed that he bought the trios' lies? At some point, he had to realize I simply could not do it. Then he got in my face and said, "I am giving you a direct order to do it!" Yeah, when pigs fly. But be it far from me not to obey an order, no, sir. I trotted off to the storage room.

Hallelujah, it was locked. So I went back and told him he needs to unlock the door. Now, the dummy didn't have a key nor did he know who did. I kept quiet, but I said, "Ask your three witnesses." I knew, but hey, he didn't ask. Someone must have told him to ask plant security. I waited by the locked door until someone opened it. The guard left. I went inside and sat down. I didn't say no, did I? I prayed and said, "God, what am I supposed to do? I need this job. I need a miracle." Fifteen minutes later, the door opened, and my partner appeared.

He said, "Brigitte, everyone in the paint room is waiting for you. They are all curious what's going to happen. I snuck away. You have to do it. I'll help you."

Did that fifty-five-gallon drum move by itself? No, of course not. Now, don't forget fifty-five gallons of rubber is heavier than paint or water. It was on a hand dolly. So to show him, not that he already knew I couldn't, I sat on the dollies handle—nothing happened. Then I held on to both handles and pulled up my feet. Nothing, not even a millimeter did the dolly budge. I truly could not do it. He then lowered the handlebars and said, "Now, you hold on to them and slowly back down the ramp." Well, that is easier said than done. When he let go of the handles, the dolly and drum launched forward, I flew a foot or so up in the air and came down with a thud. I found out later, that resulted in a slipped disc in my back.

My partner said, "Let's try it again, but this time, hold your elbows stiff and straight."

Okay, it worked. I kept everything on an even keel.

Now what we forgot to take into consideration was, first, I am going backward, and second, the dolly is going to roll down the ramp, pushing me backward. I stumbled and fell flat on my rump, the whole fifty-five-gallon drum falling on top of me. Howie, as we called him, caught it just in time so I could scoot out from underneath. I'd like to think my guardian angel was there to assist him. There were only seconds; no time for warning me. Then Howie wheeled it out of the storage room himself. He told me again, "Elbows stiff, hold it down by your hips. Walk fast so the weight doesn't shift." He took off because he didn't want anyone to see him helping me. He was afraid the evil trio also put him on their "blacklist."

That worked pretty well until a forklift truck appeared to my left. I yelled at him, "Stop, stop, stop!" He finally did. He just sat there and looked. Unfortunately, he stopped right in my path, I could only go straight. I tried to stop the dolly dead on. The liquid shifted, and the dolly came back down on me, but I held on and pushed it back up, but too much too fast. Now, I had to stop it again from touching the ground, up front. The driver's facial expression was priceless. He just shook his head. Finally, I had everything under control again. I straightened up, held my head high, smiled triumphantly, and wheeled it in the paint room toward the supervisor and the trio. Just as I came toward them, the buzzer rings, signaling the shifts end. I immediately dropped the load in front of their feet and left. It was not in the designated area. I am sure the four of them were quite capable of moving it. Let them wonder how I did it! I could have been killed several times. It wasn't my time yet.

Now, I forgot to tell you why I was being targeted. My "crime" was being transferred into the paint room. I had the seniority. I had a right to be there, right? Now, the problem was, the company planned on relocating one person from there. No problem, except the woman and one of the men were an item. She had less seniority than I had and so she was the one to go, maybe to a different shift or department. They were both married, but not to each other. Their spouses surely would have noticed if they came home two hours after their shift or left home two hours before their shift. The only time they could be together was on company time. They used to disappear in an old oven that was no longer in operation or go out in the parking lot for an hour and a half, in his car. I had to go, even if they had to kill me or cripple me.

My back injuries resulted in a workman's compensation case. The trio got rid of me; they have one person less. I had my youngest daughter with number four. She was only eighteen months old. I always wanted to be a "stay at home" mom. I got what I wanted. I was at home for five years on workman's compensation. Thanks, guys. The supervisor was eventually fired. He didn't have "common sense" and made "bad decisions." No kidding!

The First Eleventh Hour

Well, my youngest daughter's father was a gambler, alcoholic, and didn't have a real job. When I met him, he portrayed himself as a millionaire. We took trips to Puerto Rico, Saint John's, around the country, gifts, diamond bracelets, etc. Too late did I realize it was my money he was spending. Approximately $150,000. I was now broke! When I was out on workman's comp, I asked him to at least make the mortgage payments on my house. They were only $538. I figured he would at least keep a roof over our heads. He said, "That's not a problem." I just handed him the payment coupon every month. After a while, they stopped coming in the mail. Apparently, he intervened. He waited for the mail man down the street. He picked out the statements from the bank and put the rest in my mailbox. Later on, when a foreclosure notice came, he just gave it to his attorney. Somehow, he was able to defer the whole process for three years. I had no idea.

One day, I was out front playing with my girls. The neighbor from across the street came over and asked me, "How did you make out this morning with your house?"

I said, "What do you mean?" She said the house had been auctioned off this morning on the courthouse steps. Her husband had been there. I said, "You must be mistaken." I thought she was crazy. That evening, I was watching TV in the den in the back of the house. A friend and her little girl were visiting. All of a sudden, my little dog started to bark. We didn't think too much of it because she barked at the squirrels all day long. I told her to hush to no avail. Suddenly, she started to growl and run from the den through the kitchen and dining room to the living room to the front door that leads to the enclosed porch back and forth, several times. I finally got up and walked through the house, when all of a sudden, the front door opens. A lady was crouched on the floor, feeling her way around. I calmly asked, "What do you think you're doing?"

She answered, "Looking for a light switch." On the floor? I turned on the light. She said to me "What are you doing here? I thought the house was vacant."

I answered, "And why would you think that?" Of course, she told me the same thing that my neighbor had told me that morning. "Your house was auctioned off this morning." A group of investors bought it and they hired my real estate office to list it and put it on the market. My blood all went down to my toes! She showed me the papers.

Now, luckily, I noticed that the papers had used the first name of my boyfriend and the last name of my ex-husband. I said, "No such person lives here, so take your papers and leave!" I had bought the house in my name only, by myself. She left, only to return the next day. I hadn't recovered from the previous night. She handed me rephrased papers that said, "Brigitte T. Macko, other occupants, plus my dogs are to vacate the premises within seventy-two hours." I walked around like a zombie. I had twenty dollars in my pocket, a station wagon, and not much else. I would be homeless with two little girls. All furniture, clothing, toys, etc. would be gone. I didn't have the money to put it in storage. I didn't know what to do, so I did nothing. I just made breakfast for the girls, dressed them. I couldn't think.

Then the phone rang. I automatically answered it. It was my oldest daughter, Patricia. She was in the Marine Corp stationed in Okinawa, Japan. She cheerfully said, "Hi, Mom, how are you?"

I answered in a dead voice, "Fine."

"How are the girls?,"

"Fine,"

"What are you doing?"

"Nothing"

"What's wrong, Mom?"

"Nothing."

"Mom, this is me, your best friend. Tell me what's wrong, you don't sound good. You don't sound like yourself. Please, just tell me. Maybe I can help."

Finally, in an emotionally deadpan voice, I told her. I was still in shock, stunned, like the neurons in my brain short-circuited. I couldn't even cry. I told her that there was nothing she could do to help.

She said, "Are you going somewhere in the next fifteen minutes?"

"Uh, where would I go?" I had thirty hours left before I had to find out where a homeless shelter is located.

She said, "Stay by the phone. I'll call you back in fifteen minutes." True to her word she called me back in fifteen minutes and said, "Mom, I talked to dad (my first ex-husband). He is going to the court house and buying your house back for $70, 000 cash, holding a mortgage for you. Pay him as you can." I had only owed $39,000, but the closing costs, back taxes, etc. brought it up to $70,000. He didn't want me to be homeless with two little girls, five and nine, even though they weren't his. My daughter said that he said he owes you.

Now if that wasn't a miracle in the eleventh hour, I don't know what is! More like divine intervention! It was no coincidence that he was at home; cellphones weren't available in 1989. He was self-employed, and his business took him all over the North East. He usually left Syracuse on Sunday night and returned Friday night. The auction was on a Wednesday. Well, in the next five to seven years, he made $40,000 in interest, so it was a win-win arrangement. Praise the Lord!

The Vision

After I gave my youngest daughter's father, Larry, the boot, I didn't date. I only went out occasionally on Friday nights to a dance at the "One Parent Club." I didn't want a relationship with anyone. I couldn't afford it. The only thing I had done was have a correspondence with a man in jail. Somewhere in the Bible, it says, "Don't forget about the prisoners." So I thought, *Why not*. He said he had taken an expensive car for a joyride and planned to take it back but got caught before he had a chance. My thoughts were, *Well, at least he didn't kill anyone*. I went to visit two times a year for four years. He was locked up, so it was safe. Then one day, I had a strange experience. I was lying in bed, starring at the wall, thinking about him when all of a sudden, the wall moved and the paint protruded and formed his face into a white mask with horns on its head. That was my first vision. I thought it might be a sign that maybe he was evil. So I asked my oldest daughter to go online to see what she could find out. Well, he had forced his boss at gunpoint to open the safe and give him $30,000. His father lived in Florida. He hopped on the first plane to Florida where the police were waiting for him. He had shot the man in the neck, but he survived and was able to identify who shot him. He should've been on the show, *America's Dumbest Criminals*. His father's place was the first place they looked for him.

Camping Trailer Went A-WOL

In the year 2000 or so, I had bought an old camping trailer. My two youngest daughters wanted to give it a try. At first, I just bought a conversion van. We liked it; however, it didn't have the "comforts of home." We had to get up in the morning and sometimes in the middle of the night to go find a bathroom. In the mornings, I had to get dressed, go to a shower facility, get undressed, and get dressed again. We had to walk a mile to get a cup of coffee, etc. This is what led me to buy a medium-sized camping trailer.

This trailer had a tiny kitchen, a small bath-tub/shower combo and a WC. Now I could get up, make coffee, breakfast, and *then* take a leisurely bubble-bath, and only get dressed *once*. I didn't have to stand in line for any of those things—this being something we all take for granted in our homes.

In the winter months, I had the trailer in storage. Come spring, I brought it home and parked it in my driveway. That spring was no exception. As I was driving along, the trailer started to sway all over the road, rocking the van. All of a sudden, I felt a jolt. I looked to the right, and there I saw the camper veering off the road into a front lawn, down to a small brook, where it smashed into a tree/pole. My van was still going straight. I slammed on the brakes, got out, and walked toward the camper. Kitchen cupboards, dishes, plastic tumblers, silverware, bedding, you name it—everything was on the lawn. Everything crashed through the back wall of the camper. A man came running out of the house onto the front lawn. He looked like he was in shock. He was pale. He told me his whole family had been out on the front lawn playing a game of croquet just a few minutes before they had gone inside for supper.

God and their guardian angels had a hand in that. It was truly a miracle. Just the thought that a few minutes made the difference between life and death for this family. I thanked God that it hadn't happened, but this wasn't even the half of it.

My youngest daughter and her girlfriend had come along for the ride. After the camper had been hooked up, they both asked me if they could sit in the camper on the way home. At first, I of course said no because it is against the law. If a policeman saw them, I would get a ticket. Then, I thought, *Well, if we draw the drapes, then no one can see*. I was almost persuaded to say yes. They both begged me by making the cutest puppy-dog faces yet I was still undecided. In the end, I stuck with *no*. I just had this uneasy feeling about it. I couldn't tell you exactly why I said no, but had I said yes, they both would have died.

It was only about a three to four-mile trip. It seemed like such a harmless request. Just the thought of three families potentially being destroyed overwhelmed me. I sank to my knees on the lawn. I thanked God for watching over all of us. The girls just stared at the camper and all the contents of it on the lawn. I could tell they were in shock also.

My daughter finally came over, hugged me, and said, "Mom, this is the *one* time I am happy that you said no." Was everything just luck and coincidence that this family felt they just had to go in at that particular time and coincidence that I sat for a few minutes by a stop light in front of their house? Had the light been green, there would have been a very different outcome.

Usually, I would give in to my daughters' adorable puppy-dog faces. It was probably the only time I have ever said *no*. Sixth sense? Angel whisper? All I know is that it wasn't our time yet. God had timed everything down to the minute. Later on, I bought an old motor home. I thought at least nothing could get unhinged.

Interlude

Today is May 7, 2018—a beautiful, sunny day. I already took out some outdoor furniture and I thought, *Well, it's almost time to get out my outdoor kitchen.* That is when I remembered one more incident where God and the angels saved lives. I hadn't thought about that in twenty-plus years.

My daughter is typing all my handwritten a.k.a. chicken scratch pages. I talked to her on the phone a few minutes ago and told her I was done. She is praying nothing new is happening or that I don't remember more. But God is not listening to her, not yet.

I just remember two more things: Smile, from 1968 (Sorry, Carla) and one more today.

I started out to just write a booklet, but instead, it will be a book. I created a "monster" for my daughter, Carla. (Smile.)

Please Don't Cremate My Steak! (I Like It Medium-Rare)

In 1999, I was finally able to bring my two younger girls to Lockport with me. I bought a small condo near Niagara Falls, off Route 31, Wildwood Acres. I was finally able to have a moving van bring my household goods, etc.

Previously, when I was a weekend mom going back and forth from Lockport to Minoa, New York, I had just rented an unfurnished efficiency apartment. The house had ten tenants. The apartment across from me had a single male.

One day, when I had steam hissing out from underneath my car hood, he pulled up next to me. I think the radiator hose came off. He fixed it for me. We became friends. When I left, he said, "If you ever need some help with anything, let me know. You know where to find me." One day, I did.

My babysitter, a young girl, left me a note. "I can't babysit for you anymore. My boyfriend found a job and needs his car." Now what was I supposed to do? I saw the note at 8:00 a.m. and had to be back to work by 11:00 a.m. the same day. So I made the thirty-six-mile round trip and knocked on Tom's door. When he answered and opened the door, I said, "Hi, Tom! When I left, you said to me if I ever needed help with something, I could come to you. Did you mean it?"

He said, "Yes, what do you need?"

I am sure he didn't expect what I said next. Fixing a car, yes, but babysitting? I said I need someone to sleep at night with Heidi and Jennifer. To my surprise, he said yes. He did it for four years.

The first summer, I bought a new gas grill. I asked Tom to have the propane tank filled for a cookout. But he didn't have the new tank filled like I asked him. He had it exchanged for a used full one. Whoever filled that tank forgot to put a gasket on the valve.

I wheeled the grill out to the common grounds, took my long lighter, and turned the knobs on high. Whoosh! Flames shot up a foot high or more in front of my face. I quickly turned the grill off and looked. The flames still came shooting out but not out of the grill part. They came out of the top of the tank. I yelled at Tom, "Call 9-1-1!" and he did. Then I ran back into the house, only halfway up the stairs, and screamed, "*Fire!* Get out!" Then I pounded on the door to the unit on the left. A young man lived there. I yelled, "Jonathan, get out, fire!"

He answered through the door, "I can't, I just got out of the shower and I am not dressed."

I yelled, "You have two choices—get dressed and die or come out and live." He came out with only his boxer shorts on. Wise choice.

The two units to my right were occupied by the management company. After 5:00 p.m., it was empty, so I didn't bother knocking there until I saw some movement. An accountant from Florida was going over the books. The model unit was furnished. She was staying overnight in one of the bedrooms. After she came out, I looked around.

I saw my daughter, Heidi, but there was no sign of Jennifer. I asked Heidi where her sister was. She said that she didn't come down; she was still up in her bedroom playing with her Barbies. I flew back up the stairs and literally had to drag her by the hair to get her out of the house, Barbie dolls clutched in her hands. There was an unwritten rule: You simply did not disturb that child while playing with her Barbie dolls.

I went back to where the grill was, waiting for the fire department. A block or so down, a man came racing out of his unit. He quickly disconnected the tank. I don't know what he did, but it worked. He had just sat down for supper when he heard on his police scanner about the call. I asked him if he was a policeman or a firefighter. He said, "No, I just have a scanner for a hobby."

I asked why.

He said, "Lady, one more minute and that gas tank would have exploded and ripped off the whole back wall and roof of four units." The fire department hadn't arrived yet. Jennifer, Jonathan, and the accountant would have been killed.

Thank God for that man. I didn't know if it was illegal for just anyone to have a police scanner or not, but I didn't ask that question. Was it coincidence that the man had the scanner, had it on at that particular time, listened to it, and that he lived close by and made it in the nick of time? I am convinced God had a hand in it.

Both girls were mother deaf, meaning I usually had to say something at least three times before they listened. I asked Heidi, "What made you come down the first time?"

She said, "Your voice. You sounded like you were freaking out."

Well, I was.

Paranormal Activity 2004

I moved into my present home in 2004. It is unfortunately haunted. But hey, I've gotten used to it. It was normal for me. From day one, we heard noises in the attic. It sounded like a heard of elephants stomping. Then we heard voices; more like mumbling murmurs. It seemed to come from the kitchen. I joked and said, "It sounds like someone is having a party and we are not invited. How rude!" When the mumbling stopped, we heard footsteps. They stopped just before my bedroom door. Then...silence. I wasn't afraid. He never came near us.

My youngest daughter had a baby when we moved in. The closing was on August 1, 2004. Destiny was born on the tenth. I brought her home on the thirteenth. Three weeks later, my daughter went back to high school. I worked from 7:00 p.m. to 11:00 a.m., seven days a week. At 7:00 a.m., a lady came and picked up the baby (my daughter went to her classes). By 11:30 a.m., I picked up Destiny, brought her home, and fed, changed, and played with her. At 2:00 p.m., I put her in her room in her bassinet for a nap, closed the door, and then went to sleep. My daughter then came home around 3:00 p.m. She was home when Destiny woke up.

I usually slept from 2:00 to 5:30 p.m. and then woke up to make dinner and get ready for work. One day, I got up at my normal time of 5:30 p.m., and Destiny was still sleeping, or so I thought. I, of course, thought the worst. I thought she had died of that SID syndrome. She was only six months old. At that time, I had to force myself to open that door. My heart was pounding. I felt faint, but I had to. What I saw was astonishing. I couldn't move. I just stared. There she was, happily kicking her little legs, playing with her little hands and fingers, babbling softly, and looking straight at the wall. Something, someone, was entertaining her. She didn't acknowledge my presence, didn't look at me, her mobile, or her toys in the bassinet. I had to wave my hand in front of her eyes before I was able to get her attention. This happened several times. Was it her guardian angel? Some other spirit only she could see? I decided it was a "good spirit"—nothing to worry about.

Jen and I came home one evening around that time. Jen put her baby in her car seat in the TV room and placed her on the white leather couch. I stayed in the kitchen while Jen went upstairs to take a shower. I had an uneasy feeling. The house was too quiet. I decided to look in on the baby. There she was, kicking in her car seat, and the seat was sliding a little (plastic on leather). I ran out of the room, around the corner, and yelled upstairs, "Jen, get down here right now!" I wanted to show her and tell her to never do that again. I ran back into the TV room. The baby was on the couch—the seat on the floor. Without thinking, I yelled, "Jen, did you just do that?"

She said, "No, Mom! How could I? I am behind you, holding my towel around me with both hands."

Something was looking out for my little "angel" baby.

Paranormal Activity Abe Lincoln

Sometimes when I had a night off, I'd stay up to watch TV. Every time I did, around 11:30 p.m., a black shadow hovered—floated—by the fireplace. It looked like a tall, slim man with a long black coat, long tails, and a tall, old-fashioned cylinder hat. I named him Abe Lincoln.

At first, I just watched him, too surprised to say anything. Then, after a few weeks I said, "Go on to the other side. You are dead, you are not alive anymore. You don't live here. This is my house now." One night, I got mad and said, "I am not afraid of you, I am not leaving, and you are not driving me out of my own home. The house is big enough for both of us." I guess I unwillingly invited him to stay. But he was not the only nightly visitor.

I guess you could say I was the hostess with the most-est. We also heard mumbling coming from the kitchen. I talked to someone at church and told her about the nightly "parties" in my kitchen. She said the house was built in 1923. At that time, there were no funeral parlors. The dead were kept in the kitchen and displayed for family members, neighbors, friends, etc. to pay their last respects and mourn. I said, "Oh, that is just great. Now I have a corpse—dead people who think they're still alive in my house. What's next?"

My thought was that maybe "Abe Lincoln's" wife or perhaps a child had died and he is looking for them. I asked the priest from my parish to come and bless my house. We made an appointment. He was sick that day, the next appointment he had a funeral, the third appointment he had three funerals to attend. I gave up. It was not meant to be.

I took some holy water, sprinkled it all over the house, basement to attic, said the Lord's Prayer, etc. Nothing worked except I seemed to have upset something else—something more evil. One day, as I started to come downstairs, I felt my legs pulled out from under me. I expected to fall backward, but that is not what happened. I must've had something like a "blackout" (I don't drink). A few seconds later, I opened my eyes. I was staring at the carpet on a step. I was curled up in a ball, my head tucked under my chest like a turtle, nothingness again, then I came to on the bottom on the stairs. The stairs are steep, and I should've had a broken neck, at least get hurt. I was unharmed. A miracle?

This happened twice. It was like a war between a good and an evil spirit. Evil wanted me to fall down the stairs and break my neck; God saved me. I felt nothing. It was like my body had no bones. It was like a tire rolling and bouncing down the stairs. I felt nothing, I was not conscious of anything. Another miracle, you bet. Again, it wasn't my time yet.

It also happened to my granddaughter two times. She also can't explain exactly what happened. Well, evil must've lost the battle and moved on, at that time, that is.

I still wanted to help "Abe Lincoln" to go on to the other side. I went to the Historic Museum on Niagara Street. I asked a lady if she could help me find out all the names of previous owners. At first, there were only two land deeds. The house was built in 1923. Up to the 1960s something struck me as ODD. The land and the house had been sold every two (maybe four) years. It changed hands too many times up until then. Why?

The first family who stayed the longest, she recognized the name. She said that she went to school with their son and she said she will give him a call and ask if they ever heard or saw anything. The answer was no. I called the lady who sold me the house and asked—nothing. Her aunt and uncle had previously lived here for seventeen years—nothing. So why me? Why my family? Well, you know the joke: "God only knows, and he won't tell."

I had six or seven names of previous owners. So every night, when my tenant floated by the fireplace, I would say, "Mr. So-and-so, please, go on to the other side. Rest in peace." I have not seen or heard anything since, but he's still here. Several years ago, I had my friend Jeff clean up my basement. I asked him if he ever heard or saw anything. He said, "Yes, this black ghost got in my face three times. Then I finally told him to f-off." I haven't seen him since. I guess he doesn't like foul language. My daughter's girlfriend, Alysia, said something invisible tried to push her against the brick fireplace three times (it was in the daytime). She hasn't been here since.

One night, I wasn't due at work 'til 11:00 p.m. My daughter and Alysia went shopping after dinner. They had borrowed my car. At 10:00 p.m., the phone rang.

"Mom, we are at the Galleria Mall in Buffalo. We won't make it home in time. Alysia called a cab for you and a friend will come over to watch the baby."

At approximately 10:30 p.m., there was a knock on the door. A young seventeen-year-old male said he was the one Alysia called to stay with little Destiny. He sat on the couch, and at that precise moment, Abe Lincoln chose to make an earlier appearance, maybe check out this young stranger? That kid jumped up from the couch and ran out of the house so fast before I even knew what happened. I ran out after him. He was visibly shaken. He stuttered and then clenched his teeth. "Your house is haunted."

I said, "I know." Duh, *duh*, tell me something I don't know. I said it's okay, he's harmless. It took me fifteen minutes to convince him to get back inside. By then, the cab was honking by the curb. I was late for work. That young man never came back.

I had planned to go to another historic place, maybe search in archive documents, newspapers, etc. to see if an untimely death had occurred in this house, perhaps even murder. Somehow, I always had the feeling that it had something to do with a little girl, maybe five to seven years old. I never followed up on it. Stranger things happened.

Angel Vision

Between 1975 and 1979, I held a supervisory position at the General Motors plant. After only four weeks, I made a comment to my general supervisor. "If you guys keep on operating the way you do now, General Motors will close the doors here in Syracuse within ten years." Of course I was booed and laughed at, told to go home, change diapers, mop floors, etc. I lied—it took fifteen years! Well, German people were very thrifty after the war. Even if you had money, you couldn't spend it. Factories were not back in operation for civilian production. You recycled and made do with what you had. I noticed wasteful spending right off the bat. Two or three years later, the General Motors in Detroit wrote a letter. The plant has to cut their spending by nine million dollars per year or they would close the doors. I had made some suggestions earlier to cut operation expenses. My general supervisor handed them in as his own. The plant managed to save seven million dollars a year. The plant remained open for several more years. Eventually, the plant did close. The Syracuse plant did not perform a high profit margin. After all, if you only make 10 percent profit on one investment, get rid of it, and invest in something else where you can get a 20 percent return. GM is a business to make money, not cars. Making cars is just a vehicle to achieve that. I think the EDS (Electronic Data System) was one of the new investment interests.

Everyone who wanted to stay in Syracuse got a severance pay, others were transferred all over the United States. I was still out on workman's compensation. I was not notified of anything. It seemed they had forgotten about me until I got a letter from Lockport on a Wednesday to report to the Lockport plant on Monday morning at 7:00 a.m. If I didn't show up, my workman's compensation checks would stop, and it would count as a voluntary quit. I would forfeit my pension rights, blah, blah, blah. And where on Earth was Lockport? I had never heard of it. I was permanently partially disabled by the state of New York. They said they had plenty of "restricted" and "light-duty" jobs. I had four days to find a nanny for my two youngest girls. They were eight and twelve at that time.

I rolled into Lockport, New York, on a Sunday afternoon. I came to Lockport in my station wagon, a few clothes, an air mattress, and a newspaper with a "for rent" section. I was a weekend mom for ten months until a family court judge decided that I was the better parent. My ex did not pass his psychological exam. The judge told me, "Mrs. Macko, take your girls and do not walk to Lockport, run!"

For four years, I worked seven days a week, double shifts. I was able to pay back the money for the house in Minoa, New York. Nothing happened for four years. I didn't date, just worked, came home, and did the mommy thing. I turned everyone down, until one day, I had someone pursue me for four months, asking me out. I always said I was busy. Then came Easter. He made me believe that it was the first holiday he spent alone since his divorce. Yeah, what divorce? So my soft-hearted self invited him for Easter dinner along with two other male friends and a new neighbor. That was Easter Sunday. On Wednesday, he showed up at my home and said, "Now that we are dating, I want a commitment, buy you a ring, then get married."

I said no and I said I didn't know we were dating. Huh? What are you smoking in your pipe? He didn't give up. He was persistent and finally wore me down. He showed up at my workstation every single day. He did a fine job of selling himself. I can retire, do your grocery shopping, cook, show up for your daughter to after-school activities, cut the grass, etc., etc., etc. He was going to help me out and be Mr. Wonderful. Well, I thought I'd give it a try. After all, I had nothing else to do at the moment, but if something sounds too good to be true, it usually is.

I didn't really want another man in my life, but it sounded so good, so I said okay, I'd give it a try. It didn't exactly sound too enthusiastic, but we looked for a larger home. We were supposed to each put $10,000 down, split the mortgage payments, heat and food bill, etc. That, of course, didn't happen nor did anything else he promised. Three weeks before the wedding, he moved in with me. That is when I discovered he was a nasty violent drunk. Also, his divorce had not been finalized; he nor his wife had paid the attorney or filing fees. I paid for everything—approximately $15,000. Then he wanted a camping trailer to go to Syracuse for the state championship for the flying disc competition. He had won it a few years earlier. Now, here is a guy that drinks gin until he passes out, gets up, and hits a flying object out of the air. I mean, gin in the noodle soup? I was afraid of him. I did everything he asked just to keep him from getting mad in a drunken stupor. My daughter and I had a plan in case it looked like he was going to hit one of us. One runs out the front door, the other out the side door. I figured he can only chase one of us. One evening, we ran out, hopped in my car, and spent the night in a motel in Niagara Falls. When we returned at noon the next day, a state trooper was there. He had reported us missing. He insisted on driving me to work every night and then went out drinking. I told him I did not want him to drive me anywhere while he's drunk. One night, we argued on the way. He insisted he wasn't drunk. Yeah, right. In the morning, he failed to show up. So I walked six miles home to Pendleton. When I arrived home, the phone was ringing. He was in overnight jail and his truck had been impounded. He wanted me to pick him up. I refused. I had just walked home for six miles, I figured he could do the same. He was drinking at the Niagara hotel, saw a policeman walk in the front door, and ran out the back door and jumped in his truck. Instead of driving away, he accidentally put it in reverse and hit the police cruiser head on, but of course, he wasn't drunk.

After that, I took my own car again. He also always pressured me to let my youngest daughter's father have custody. There would be more time and money for him. He was mean to her and woke her up in the middle of the night just to tell her that her dad was a drunk. One time, she retorted back, "And what are you?"

He told me she should be disciplined. I said, "What for? For speaking the truth?"

After that, he did everything he could to upset her. First, he killed her little dog and told us it ran away, but I noticed that the woodpile looked like it had been somewhat rearranged. When I checked it out, I found blood and black hair on them. Then we got a cat. It also disappeared. He also ran away—not! He is probably at the bottom of the Erie Canal. He told me once that his ex-wife had nine cats. He said he broke their necks and put them in the canal. Then some kid gave her a kitten. That was short-lived.

One morning, I heard a blood-curdling scream from my daughter's bedroom. I rushed in. Next to her head was the dead kitten. I could tell that the neck had been broken by the way that the neck was bent back. He said that my daughter was fat and put her fat body on top of the kitten in her sleep and crushed it to death. Oh yeah? I suppose the dead kitten crawled up next to her face.

After that, we gave up on having any kind of pet. My daughter was traumatized plus I didn't want another pet to die. Besides, I was afraid I would find my daughter in bed one morning with a broken neck. He had "blackouts."

Then he started to haunt me to give up custody of my daughter because her father didn't pay child support. He said he had to pay, so why shouldn't he? That was a lie. He had given up his paternal rights so he wouldn't have to pay child support. I surmised no one ever nominated him for father of the year award. Eventually, he threatened to throw my daughter out the window. I thought it was funny at first. It was a ranch-style home with extremely low windows, maybe three feet off the ground, and bushes underneath. His threats progressed to "I am going to kill her." Now that wasn't funny. I was scared to death. That's when supernatural things started to happen. The kitchen cabinet started to slam open, shut, open, shut, etc. When I got up to check, there was no one there. I finally realized that it always happens ten minutes before Ron returned home, something wanted us to know, to be awake when he came home so I could evaluate the situation; was he in a violent mood or passing out? It was not uncommon for him to pass out before he came in. In the backyard, garage, etc. He was too heavy for me to move inside, so I left him wherever. At some point, we had ignored the door slamming. The next thing we knew, the smoke alarm and the heat detector started to go off simultaneously. We rushed out, but nothing. Again, only ten minutes before he walked in the door. It was odd. It was like a warning signal, "danger approaching."

One time, I wanted him to get some dry wood from the wood pile to start a fire in the fireplace. I told him to make sure the flute was open. Yeah, you guessed it. He didn't know which end was up. The flute was closed, the whole room looked like it was covered in a white foggy cloud. Our eyes were biting, burning, and irritated. He finally took the tongs and threw the burning log out into the snow. The fire detector and heat detector, located on the ceiling above the fireplace, never went off. So I know that was also a sign from above—to be alert when he comes home. After he had threatened to kill my daughter, I told him he had to leave. He said he would kill himself then if another woman rejects him.

My daughter said, "Yeah, let him." I was afraid he'd take his Magnum 44, put it in his mouth, and blow out his brains in my daughter's bedroom on her bed so she would be the one to find him. His last dirty deed to traumatize her.

I started to pray day and night. "Heavenly Father, tell me what to do, should I kill him first before he kills my child?" I don't want to commit murder—take someone's life. If it was me who was threatened, I would wait and see what happens. But if I die or go to jail, my daughter would be an orphan and go into a foster home. So I kept praying. Soon after that, I constantly saw some black spot to my right. I kept turning my head to the right so often I was afraid my coworker thought I had Tourette's syndrome.

Strange things were happening at home again. Jennifer and I went in the bathroom together one night. All of a sudden, the lights flickered. We were stunned. We looked at each other. I said to her, let's see if it happens again." I said, "If there is a good spirit present, please flicker the lights three times." It did, and we were speechless. We were spellbound. I said, "Let's try it in the great room." I had a five-arm floor lamp. One lightbulb was black and burnt out. We sat down, and again, I repeated it. "If there is a good spirit in this house, please click the lights on three times." What happened was only the burned-out lights flickered on and off. I couldn't believe it. I turned the lamp off and on myself, but only the four good ones came on; the fifth stayed dark. I checked the burnt-out bulb and put it on each of the four other sockets —nothing. That bulb was burnt out. We were finally convinced that there was a good spirit in the house. But I kept asking Ron to leave; he wouldn't. Eviction and restraining orders wouldn't do any good. I was afraid that would just make him stark raving mad and shoot us both. I continued to pray, "God, please give me a sign what to do."

One evening, just as it was starting to get dark, out of nowhere, an angel appeared in front of me. I wanted to call to my daughter, but I was paralyzed from head to toe. I couldn't speak. I couldn't move a muscle. It was a beautiful lady, honey-colored wavy hair, blue eyes, long white dress surrounded by a bright white unnatural light, almost blinding. I can't remember if she had wings or bnot. I just stared at her face. She smiled, nodded her head, and it was as if I heard Angel-whisper-thought-transfer, whatever it was, say, "Everything will be all right." And she disappeared.

After that, when I asked Ron to leave, I felt at peace, the words "everything will be all right" appeared in my brain. Two weeks later, I had asked him to leave again. At least two to three years had passed. He said the same thing, no, but this time, he added, "I don't want to live alone." Bingo! I don't know why I said what I said now; it was like something I normally would never have said.

"Why don't you look for someone else while you still live here?"

That is what he did. God gave me the answer.

One time, my daughter Carla had called to let us know that she and her sister Heidi would come from Syracuse to spend Christmas with us. She was on the phone with my youngest daughter. Ron came home, and right away, he started harassing and yelling at Jennifer. Carla was still on the phone, so she heard everything. They arrived sometime during the afternoon. Later in the evening, I said, "Well, you two can sleep on the two couches."

Carla said, "No, we are going to a motel. We stopped and paid for a room before we came to the house. I heard him on the phone just once. We refuse to spend even one night under the same roof with him." It broke my heart. My two daughters wouldn't even spend Christmas with me because of him.

The Second Eleventh Hour

You are never forgotten.

If you ever feel that no one is thinking about you, you are dead wrong. Try not paying your taxes to the IRS. They haven't forgotten you. It is a living nightmare, but you can't wake up and make it go away. At first, I did nothing after my retirement. I just watched TV, read books, and became a couch potato. After a few months, I became bored. My youngest daughter had a baby at sixteen. She went back to high school after the baby was only three weeks old. I was working the graveyard shift and took care of the baby during the day, my daughter taking care of her at night. For some strange reason, the baby kept waking up, crying half the night at10:00 p.m., 12:00 a.m., and 4:00 a.m.

After 4:00 a.m., my daughter couldn't go back to sleep, so she stayed up. She fed, changed, and played with her, then stayed up and got ready to go to school. The bus came at 7:00 a.m. She quit school in April. She said she used to fall asleep in school with her head on her desk. When the bell rang, she didn't wake up right away and heard the other kids making fun of her and debating if they should wake her up or let her sleep. She was embarrassed and didn't go back. I told her she couldn't just sit around and do nothing. She had to get a job. No one would hire her, not even as a dishwasher. I had this idea to start a commercial cleaning business because you don't need a diploma for that. I spent $25,000 cash to buy into a franchise business to give her a job. She did okay, but then I had to watch the baby while she worked and then go clean my own accounts late at night. So I decided to do all the accounts myself and had her take classes to get her GED. She passed but still couldn't get hired. I assume that most employers thought she might miss a lot of time because of the child.

One of her girlfriends suggested to her that she get her CNA diploma—certified nurse's assistant. She also passed and is working for the past ten years or so up to seventy hours a week, twenty-nine days in a row, fourteen hours a day. My business took off faster than I imagined. I had to pay my own taxes. I had seven part-time employees. I am a sucker for the underdog. I paid them under the table. Some were retired, some on disability, some just out of drug rehab, jail, and so on. I tried to give them a hand up. I knew I was responsible for the taxes on the money I paid them. So I went to my tax preparer.

He looked at the first three columns, shoved everything back across his desk, and said, "You have to go home and get receipts, documentation, etc. for these three items."

I asked him, "How and where do I get these?"

He said he didn't know but to start at work and call and ask who takes care of retirees. I called and left messages. No answer, no one called back. So finally, I went there only to be told the lady retired two months after I did, and the position was not being replaced. Now what? I finally made phone call after phone call, and by October that year, I was able to get the documents I needed. So I thought I might as well wait and do it together the following year. When I did, the tax man said, "That is all well and good, but now you need three more documents." I had no idea how to get them or what to do. I asked someone at the UAW Hall. They gave me some phone numbers to try.

Again, it was fall before I was able to get what I needed. I went to the tax preparer's home where there was a sign, "Oxygen in use." I knocked on the door, and his wife answered. She told me that he has lung cancer and does not feel up to working. Their out-of-town son would be here next tax season. So I left, and then the man died, but his son didn't take over. So now what? They had all my previous tax returns for the past ten years. I still had six properties left in the Syracuse area. My long form was inches thick. You just don't go in and out and get it done in thirty minutes and walk out with a check in your hand.

While I was employed at General Motors, I usually had $8,000 to $9,000 coming back, loss of rents, taxes, mortgage, interest, insurance, etc. on the income properties. After retirement, I sold all six properties. I couldn't afford five mortgages anymore. My tenants also lost their jobs, got divorced, one died, etc. Of course, the IRS now also wanted capital gain taxes. What capital gain? I sold one house for the same price I bought it for forty years ago. Some for less than what I paid for. I actually believed I had a return coming. Yeah, right. No such luck.

Anyway, I didn't know what to do. Every time I don't know what to do, I do what I do best—nothing, smile. While I did nothing, I became ill. I had unexplainable diarrhea. At first, I thought, *Great, at least I'll lose some weight*. After three weeks, I finally decided to see my doctor. It obviously wasn't just a twenty-four-hour bug or virus that should have worked itself out. After some tests, results came in, and I found out I had an intestinal bacterial infection. My doctor prescribed antibiotics, one pill for ten days. By day five, I still had my original problem, and now I had a new problem—vomiting violently. I mean, my stomach felt like an erupting volcano and the other end like Niagara Falls. I lay down on my bathroom floor. I couldn't get up and couldn't lift my head. I think it was vertigo on top of it. My phone was on top of my bathroom vanity. I couldn't drag myself up to reach it and call for help.

After a few hours, I felt a little better, cleaned myself up, and went to the emergency room. I only lived one block from the hospital. They gave me another antibiotic via IV. By 8:00 a.m., I was released with another prescription. Another ten-day treatment. Again, by day five, I broke out in hives. My whole body was covered with little red dots, itching like mad. I scratched and scratched. It drove me crazy. I felt like every root of my hair was hurting, little blisters forming, etc. By evening, I couldn't stand it anymore and went back to the ER. Another IV treatment and another prescription. By day five, the hives came back. Another trip to the ER, another five days, and I'm sure you guessed it, another problem. This time, my throat closed up. I couldn't breathe. There was no time to call for an ambulance. I grabbed my car keys, flew out the door, jumped into my car, and raced to the hospital in two minutes flat. This time, I was admitted and taken upstairs to a room. The antibiotics worked, but I was dehydrated and weak. Diarrhea and nausea persisted. When a nurse cranked up the back of my bed so I was in a sitting position, I just slumped down. I couldn't even sit up. Now they gave me steroids to build up my muscles. I still had some trouble breathing and was given oxygen. That didn't seem to help. I felt like an elephant was sitting on my chest. After complaining about that for three or four days, they finally took some x-rays. I had pneumonia.

After eight days in the hospital, eating and drinking very little, I only had one shower. I was told they were too busy. My hair looked like I fell into a can of Crisco, greasy. I felt I smelled like a septic tank. I couldn't stand myself. I told the hospital physician, "I am going home." He said he couldn't release me yet, I was still too sick. He said I didn't realize it, but I could have died. Well, I guess it just wasn't my time yet again. He also said that I could only get the antibiotics that worked for me while I was in the hospital. They cost $700 and my insurance only covers while I am admitted. I told him I don't care, I'll pay for it out of my pocket. I asked him to give me the prescription and signed myself out. Needless to say, he was not a happy camper. He also gave me something to wean myself off the steroids. I walked out of there with wooden legs. Due to the steroids, my muscles felt tight, like they were bursting through my skin. I went to the pharmacy walking like I was on stilts. They said they didn't have them on hand. They had to order them. It'd take twenty-four hours. The next day, I went back. They handed me my prescription. Instead of $700, they only charged me my regular $4 copay. I didn't question it. I figured my insurance is paying for them after all. Yeah right. They were generic, but I didn't know that. Well, the hives came back. This time, I didn't go back to the ER. I went to see my doctor instead. He said I am allergic to the antibiotic, but he'll try something else. There are supposedly 234 different antibiotics. I now know I am allergic to seven of them. I'll have 227 to try out the next time I get sick. Well, it was another ten-day treatment. I half expected to have another reaction by day five. All went well until day eight. I felt it itching again, but nothing else happened. During this time, I forgot all about the IRS, but the IRS didn't forget about me. The nasty letters arrived. I still didn't know who to go to. Every time I went to work or shopping, I expected my house to be locked and boarded up courtesy of the IRS.

Then one day, my oldest daughter, Patricia, called just to say hi! She doesn't call very often, just at the right time, the eleventh hour. I don't think it was a coincidence. Something told her to call Mom for no particular reason for the second time. It must have been an angel whisper. I was depressed and she picked up on it. I said, "If I kill myself, will you come to my funeral?"

She was very compassionate and said, "I can't stop you from two to three thousand miles away, why don't you tell me what your problem is? Maybe I can help."

So I told her. She said, "Well, when I was stationed in Hawaii, our office did the taxes for 2000 Marines and retirees. Send me everything you have."

So I did. A few days later, she called back and said, "Thanks, Mom. I just had a nightmare delivered to my desk," and hung up. It took her probably two years and two transfers to get everything she needed and numerous phone calls to who-knows-where. In the meantime, the letters became more threatening. I already saw myself homeless. So I called one of these tax attorneys. Now, they don't do your taxes, they just make an agreement with the IRS to resolve the problem. They charged $17,500 for the service. In the meantime, I had to pay $700 a month toward my arrears. In the meantime, my daughter finally got all the necessary documents except one. While I was a supervisor for General Motors for three years, I signed up for the stock program. We got paid twice a month. I signed up to take out $50 each paycheck toward stocks. At that time, it was $45 a share. Whatever was left, I had them hold on to, plus my dividends, and buy more. At one time, the stocks were $90 each. At $90, they split. When I went back to hourly, I stopped but kept and didn't cash them in until I retired.

Now, the IRS wanted to know exactly how much I paid for each share. I had no idea. I never saw a stock certificate nor did I know how much exactly they went up or down. I was told that I was supposed to have saved my pay stubs. Who keeps their pay stubs for forty years? I had 1,100 shares. We called Fidelity Investments, electric data Investments, ETC General Motors in Detroit, etc. and were told they only kept records for nine years. I cashed the stocks after retirement at $43 a share. Less than I paid for. I figured I have a loss to deduct. I paid between forty-five and ninety. My daughter just figured, put down $78, and they accepted it. If you lie to their advantage, it's acceptable. The whole mess took three years to clean up. Now I have to pay $700 a month as well as another $600 a month. $1,300 was a hardship. The arrears were reduced to $350, but it'll take twice as long. Not only do they charge you interest but also late fees. A double whammy. But instead of the original $117,000, I only owed $57,000. I did get credit for some of my deductions. Lucky me. Coincidence that Patty called at the right time? She didn't call very often and still doesn't. My second eleventh hour had occurred.

Angel Whispers in My Front Yard

First Incident

It's a good thing my guardian angels are watching out over me 24/7. A psychic told me once that I have four, all archangels, high up in rank. This, she said, is highly unusual. Their names are Michael, Gabriel, Uriel, and Haiciel. They probably take turns. I am too much for just one to handle.

One day, I decided to rake up some leaves in my backyard. I had two rakes. One had a broken handle. I chose the one with the shorter handle at first. I figured it was easier and lighter to hold. The top of the handle cut into my palm, so I leaned it up against the fence, went into the garage, and used the new one to get back to work.

The neighbor had a huge maple tree. Most of it was hanging over the fence, and of course, all the leaves came down into my yard. All of a sudden, I thought I heard someone say, "Pick up that rake." I turned around. The broken rake had fallen over.

I hesitated and thought, *Why would I even bother to pick up that rake? I am only going to put it in the garbage when I am done.*

Again, something whispered a little more forcefully, "Go pick up that rake."

So I walked away, still wondering why I even bothered doing it. It seemed like something stupid to do. I can't explain why I did it—I just did.

I picked up the rake and leaned it up against the fence again. It toppled over. I bent down, picked it up, and made sure I placed it at just the right angle so it wouldn't fall over again. All the while, I was wondering why I was doing this. I didn't really care if this rake stood up or fell down. It felt strange somehow. What I really felt like doing was breaking it up into pieces so it would fit into my garbage can.

Once I was satisfied that the rake would stand up straight, I turned around. As I did, I stopped dead in my tracks. It took a few seconds for me to comprehend what I saw. A huge branch had broken off that tree at the same spot where I was standing one minute earlier. There was no doubt in my mind a miracle had occurred. What I heard was no earthly whisper. Had I not walked away, I would have been dead.

It just wasn't my time yet.

Second Incident

Another time, perhaps another year, I psyched myself up to cut the grass. I had a phobia about it. I always feared I would cut off my toes. Sometimes, I even wore steel-toed shoes.

I pushed the lawnmower down the long driveway around my house and started it in the front yard, close to the house, and pushed it back and forth, toward the sidewalk. On the other side of the sidewalk, there was a small strip of grass before the road. That strip of grass allegedly belongs to the city, but homeowners have the privilege of cutting it. If you don't, the city will give you a $300 fine for not taking advantage of that privilege.

Toward the end of my property line, there was a huge old tree. I estimated it at least around a hundred years old. Gnarly old roots protruded out of the ground. It was hard to cut the grass around the tree. So of course, I did the easy part first, back and forth only twice from my driveway to the tree. The grass strip was only two lawnmowers width wide.

Once that part was done, I stood under the tree, debating whether or not I should just finish tonight or quit and do it in the morning. Now, mind you, the rest was only two lawnmowers wide, at the most fifteen feet long to my neighbor's property. Who in their right mind doesn't finish in the same day and instead gets the lawnmower out again in the morning? I just had an uneasy feeling about finishing. I couldn't explain it. It hadn't started to rain, I didn't expect company, I had no places to go shopping or visit anyone, etc. All I planned to do was put on my swimsuit, lie in my lawn chair, and work on my suntan in the backyard, maybe cool off a little in the pool.

For some strange reason, I walked away thinking how dumb that was. I almost turned around to finish, but I didn't.

The next morning, I took my lawnmower and walked back out front. A huge branch (actually it looked more like half a tree) had broken off and laid across the sidewalk into my front yard. It had missed the house. I hadn't heard a voice the day before, just an eerie feeling not to finish. My dumb decision probably saved my life again.

I called the city. After all, it was their tree. It had to be completely removed. It had a tree disease.

Was it luck? I doubt it.

Evil Lurks Close By

December 30, 2006

I am sure everyone is familiar with the phrase "Hear no evil, see no evil, speak no evil." Please take it seriously. I wish I had. I wish that my mouth had been cemented shut that night. It started on the evening when I watched the hanging of Saddam Hussein on TV. The henchmen folded a napkin around his neck and put the noose over it. I thought, *Good riddance.* When it was over, I watched the commentary hour. When they said the napkin around his neck was to prevent a "rope burn mark" from the noose because he was their leader, and when his followers went to pay their last respects, they wouldn't want to see the mark. Wow, put a bag over his head and shoot the followers. Hello! We are talking about a mass-murderer, Hitler's evil twin. He killed his daughter, son-in-law, and five-year-old grandson. They had fled to Afghanistan. When he found out where they lived, he gassed the whole village. And he deserves consideration? I raved and ranted out loud, "Hanging was too good for the S.O.B. He should have been tortured with bamboo sticks put under his fingernails, beaten, laid on a board with spiked roofer's nails, and thrown in a shark tank." Saddam Hussein had devised 107 torture techniques. He made Hitler look like an altar boy.

Afterward, I went to bed still upset. I couldn't fall asleep, so I just stared at the ceiling. All of a sudden, there was Saddam Hussein's face, beet red, with horns on his head. He looked like the devil. I stared. I couldn't move; I could only watch. The face floated an inch or two down from the ceiling. Back up, back down, a little further this time, back up, and back down, getting closer and closer to me. My heart started to beat faster. I got scared. I closed my eyes, the vision still appeared. Now my heart was racing, beating like a drum. I thought I would explode and have a heart attack. I finally got up and ran into every room, up and down, turned on all the lights, grabbed the phone, and called my daughter, Jennifer, and told her what happened. I half expected her to laugh at me, call me crazy, or complain I woke her up at 2:00 am.

The only theory I can come up with is that when I had said all those evil things about torturing Saddam Hussein, the devil must have thought he found a kindred spirit, an evil soul, and he wanted me to be with him. Again, it wasn't my time. But the devil is persistent. He, just like Jesus, wants to win souls. If he wins, he would reign over the world someday, and we would all burn in the fires of hell for eternity.

Sometime later, I also couldn't fall asleep and stared at the ceiling. In the summer heat, the asphalt throws up heat and it looks like the air is moving in waves. That is what I'm seeing up on the ceiling; black air moving in ripples. I thought my eyes were playing tricks on me, closed my eyes, rolled over, said my Lord's Prayer, and prayed for all my deceased relatives and fell asleep. That happened a few more times. Then, one night, the waves looked like bats flapping their wings. I ignored it, rolled over, and went to sleep. The devil doesn't like to be ignored, obviously.

But I still wasn't afraid, so he had to get my attention somehow and in some other way. The next time the bats appeared, flapping their wings, it looked like 1000 bats with one difference. They each had two eyes staring down at me. The eyes were the most unnatural evil eyes, a deep gold-green color, like maybe comparable to a tiger. They never came closer though, just staring down at me menacingly. I slept with the light on for a while.

Secret Wishes, Instant Answers!

A few years ago, I leafed through some advertisements in the newspaper. I wasn't looking for anything in particular. I didn't need anything, didn't want anything, and couldn't afford anything. I didn't have any credit cards; I was a strict "cash and carry" girl.

When I was twenty-one, I bought my first car back in Germany—a brand new Volkswagen Beetle—in cash. Up until then, I walked everywhere. When we came here to the USA, my first husband couldn't find a job in Oswego, New York. He took a job with Air-Asia, based in Thailand. I was supposed to follow, so I decided to sell the Beetle. My mother-in-law put an ad in the paper. One day, she said, "Brigitte, you have a phone call." A man asked about the car for his son. Of course, he asked how much. I told him the same price I paid in Germany sixteen months earlier. That was still cheaper than he would have had to pay here. He said he'd take it.

Then he asked, "How did you pay for it?"

I replied, "With money." Secretly, I thought *Duh. What kind of moron am I dealing with? What else do you think the dealer took?*

Again, he asked, "How did you pay for the car?" A little frustrated, I thought it might be a prank call.

I answered, "With money."

He asked, "Where did you get the money from?"

"The bank."

"How did you finance it?"

Now, I had only been in the country for four months. My vocabulary was very limited. Words like financing, credit, payments, etc., were foreign to me. Cash was all I was familiar with. Until I was maybe sixty-eight or so, I didn't own credit cards.

So when I read that ad about a piece of Blackwood furniture, I thought, *Just like my oma's living room and dining room set. I just have to have it.* Now, that piece of furniture was a dry bar. I needed a dry bar like I needed a hole in my head. What to do with it?

I had no idea—still don't. It is still in my kitchen. The problem was the bar sold in "fine furniture" stores for $900 or at the Bargain Outlet for $300.

But that day, you could spin a wheel and get from 5 percent to 50 percent off. I had no credit card and only $200 cash to my name at that time. My utility bill just had to wait.

I called my friend, Jeff; he owned a truck. After all, I needed to get it to my house. I explained to him why and that there is a possibility I have to embarrass myself and tell the cashier, "Sorry, I don't have enough money." Now, how sane was that? I still can't believe I did that.

On the way to the store, I felt elated. I said in my mind, "Jesus, I have to hit that 50 percent mark." Somehow, I just knew I would. When we got there, the arrow was at 40 or 45 percent. I just gave it a little push.

The cashier said, "You have to spin that wheel around at least one time."

I was nervous. I asked Jeff to do it. He said, "No, this is your call" and disappeared to the back of the store. He didn't want to be embarrassed either.

So I gave the wheel a hard push and watched it go slower, slower, and slower, my eyes fixed on the 50 percent. I was holding my breath, anxious to see where it would stop. I couldn't believe my eyes! The arrow pointed at 50 percent. I let out a yell. "Jeff! I hit 50 percent!" I couldn't see him anywhere. I paid for it—$150 plus tax.

I felt overjoyed. I had my dry wine bar and a few dollars in my pocket. While Jeff loaded the big box into his truck, I headed for home. I was on cloud nine. I came to a stoplight. I was impatiently waiting for the light to turn green. I looked to my left, and I saw a car speeding down the road. And I thought, *Well, by the time he gets to the light, he'll have red and he'll stop."* The light turned green, and I immediately put my foot on the gas pedal.

A voice in my head said, "Don't go, this car will not stop." I hesitated and stopped. That car didn't. He actually accelerated. Had I not stopped, he would have hit me right on the driver's side—a T-bone crash. He could have killed me. I was in shock. I knew I had another angel whisper. It wasn't my time yet.

Like I said earlier, I kept my guardian angel very busy. It wasn't my time yet!

Highway to Heaven

I felt like somehow I had found communication with God. I call it my highway to heaven. Did I stop asking for favors? Of course not; I just asked it silently. I have an inquiring mind.

I was forced to retire from GM and had started a commercial cleaning business and hired a few part-time employees, but I cleaned a few businesses myself. Of course, that meant "after hours." A few days a week, I cleaned three places myself, starting at 5:00 or 6:00 p.m., coming home around midnight.

One day after Thanksgiving, I came home, and while I turned into my driveway, I heard the first Christmas song on the radio that year. I sat there and finished listening to the song, my favorite—"Silent Night." I put my head on the steering wheel, tears flowing down my cheeks. I was homesick and missed my oma. I silently said, "I know it's not possible, but I wished I could be your little girl again for just one more Christmas Eve, have you hold my hand while we trudge through the ice and snow on the sidewalk to go to midnight Christmas Mass, and sing 'Stille Nacht, Heilige Nacht.'" I continued my one way conversation and I thought, *Oma, and while I'm at it, could you please ask God to let you give me a sign that you are happy and in heaven? Something specific, so I could recognize it, that the message is from you? Amen.*

Well, my oma always started her Christmas cut-out butter cookies at least six weeks before Christmas. She said it brings out the buttery flavor and the vanilla extract. They needed to cure, something like that.

So a few days later, I said to myself, "You ought to go down to the basement and get the cookie sheets." They were stored down there in plastic bins. That went on for several days; all I did was say to myself, "You ought to go down there." The thought was like a nagging thorn in my side. So finally, I did. I went downstairs as if on autopilot and made a left. I looked around, somewhat confused, and thought, *What are you doing here? The cookie sheets are in the room to the right.* I turned around to go back out. That is when I saw a small silver chain-link blinking like a little star on the dirty basement floor.

By dirty, I mean dirty. There had been several floods down there and no sub pump, the water just slowly evaporating and leaving the dirt behind.

At first, I almost walked away, but just like always, something just made me do it. I grabbed a wire coat hanger and removed the dirt very cautiously. Why? I don't know. It's highly unlikely that it was going to bite me. I uncovered one chain link, then another and another and another and so on. Usually, chain links are round circles. These were oblong, obviously handmade. I still didn't have any idea what it was until I got to the end. It was a silver dollar from 1879. I recognized it immediately. My oma had given it to me when I was sixteen. She was born in 1879 and so was her husband. His parents were from Germany, came to Philadelphia, had a son, and returned to my hometown when he was five years old. He became a gold and silversmith and made a mounting around it and a chain.

I was elated. Oh my god. This was definitely a distinctive object-sign that this was from my oma—that she is happy and in heaven.

I cleaned it up and pressed it to my heart. I was so happy it made my heart sing. What was the miracle? That pendant had been stolen forty years ago. I hadn't seen it in 40 years, 200 miles away. That wasn't something you could buy at Walmart. Only I would recognize it. I was on cloud nine.

I forgot all about the cookie sheets and cookies. I had something more precious. A few days later, I had the same nagging thoughts, *You really, really ought to go downstairs and get those cookie sheets.* Again, I went downstairs, turned left, and didn't know what I was doing there. I thought, *Well, I am seventy.* I was concerned I must have signs of dementia. I turned around to turn off the light and I saw a small glittering in the dirt again. I slowly fished it out of the dirt and I was dumbfounded.

It was another pendant that my oma had given me at sixteen, at the same time as the silver dollar necklace; I couldn't believe my eyes. I walked upstairs in a daze. I cleaned it up. It was somewhat worn—the figure and lettering, numbers, etc., were hard to see, but I knew what it was. It wasn't an old coin. It was a religious medallion. It had Mother Mary and Baby Jesus sitting on a cloud on one side. It says, "Madonna Baveriae (Bavaria)." I couldn't decipher the other side, but I remember the story behind it.

My great-grandfather had a small grocery store, fresh produce included. The climate in Germany wasn't warm enough to grow citrus fruit such as oranges and lemons. So once a year, he walked through Germany, Bayern included (Bavaria), Austria, and Italy to get oranges and lemons. He had a large woven basket that went from head to toe, which he carried on his back like a backpack. It usually took him three to four months.

That was his talisman, his medallion for protection. I was so stunned and happy I could've died or jumped over the moon. There was no good explanation to how these things came to be in that basement.

Then I remembered something I read someplace, possibly the Bible. I am not sure about that. I can't quote it word for word but "God returns stolen items and makes jewels appear." Well, these items were stolen and returned; they were not jewels, but they meant more to me than the Krupp Diamond. (That was the largest diamond at the time, owned by the Krupp family in Germany. Elizabeth Taylor owned it later on.)

Now, I've had electricians down there, plumbers, two roto-rooter men, and friends who had started to paint the walls with waterproof paint for me. I asked my friend, Dave, if he ever saw anything while working in that part of the basement. He said no.

Well, I honestly can't remember if I ever retrieved those cookie sheets or even baked cookies that year. Life goes on.

Dove or Pigeon?

That is the question.

In the Catholic faith, we believe in the Trinity: Holy Father, Jesus the Son, and the Holy Ghost or Spirit.

In one of my prayers, I say, "Jesus, come into my heart, Holy Spirit put love into my soul." Now the Holy Spirit is always portrayed as a white dove. One day, I was upstairs in my bathroom, brushing my teeth. As I was bent over the sink, I heard a slight sound, maybe like a little bird chirping. I didn't pay too much attention at first. The sound got louder and louder and louder. I am 50 percent hearing impaired and for me to hear it, it had to be extra loud. It was persistent. By now, it sounded like shrieking. I thought, *What in the world is that?*

I finally looked out the window. I expected a whole flock of birds fighting and pecking at each other with their beaks, feathers flying, and dead birds in my backyard.

But that is not what I saw. One—only one—white bird frantically flying from my pine tree to my garage roof and from the roof back to the tree, back and forth, coming closer to the window every time, at least fifteen to twenty times. It was eerie, almost scary, like at any moment, that white bird would come crashing through the window.

I followed the bird back and forth with my eyes. At one time, it seemed we made eye contact, but still, it flew back and forth, shrieking like a banshee.

Then I felt an electric-like shock going through my brain, and two words came to mind—Holy Spirit. Now I got it. The Holy Spirit wanted to make its presence known to me. As soon as I realized that, the bird disappeared.

God sometimes communicates with us through animals. I don't know if that bird was a white dove or a pigeon. I can't tell the difference. All I know is that the wings were white and spread out like an eagle's.

Channel Surfing

I had gotten into the habit of watching TV at night, only a few channels. Soon, there were only reruns on. So I went channel surfing. During that time, I had that eerie feeling that I should "do something for the glory of God." Who? Me? I was just a simple little old lady, what could I possibly do?

That thought stayed with me for three or four years. I couldn't think of anything. I did start watching HGTV at midnight. *International House Hunters*. They featured beautiful multi-million dollar vacation homes around the world in the Virgin Islands, Italy, France, Africa, the Greek Islands, Morocco, etc.

One day, I thought, if I had the money, where would I go? And would I even want to? What would I do there all by myself? Would my girls go with me? Nah, they have their own lives to live.

One night, I only heard one word—Jerusalem. Where did that come from? I had never even thought or considered that possibility, what does it mean? Should I go there for a ten-day pilgrimage, move there, what?

A week or two later, I discovered TCT. And what was the first program I stumble onto? The International Fellowship between Christians and Jews. Rabbi Eckstein was featured in Russia, bringing meals and winter clothing to the elderly and sick Holocaust survivors. He was asking to help those poor people to get out of Russia to the homeland—Israel, relocating to Jerusalem. The living conditions just broke my heart. I thought that if I was Jewish, my lifelong dream would have been to return to the Promised Land. Even if I died on board the plane, I would at least be buried there, my final resting place would be in the Holy Land.

So I signed up for the "Wings of Eagles." Coincidence? Starting with *International House Hunters*? Maybe? Maybe not!

However, I did not have that "Aha, this is it" moment. I just renewed my passport, December 2016, just in case it'll come to me, whatever it is I am supposed to do, so I'll be prepared.

A few weeks later, I was channel surfing again in the morning. I came upon the 700 Club helping the needy around the world. Children and women, walking ten miles one way, carrying large containers on their heads, going to watering holes to get dirty, muddy drinking water. I couldn't imagine anyone having to live like that. It tugged on my heartstrings. I felt blessed. So I became a member. I thought maybe I am just supposed to help less fortunate people.

I remembered reading "Jesus said, whatever you do unto them, you do unto me." I'll get my reward in heaven.

High-Flying Books

My oma was constantly on my mind. We had a special bond that just couldn't be broken even after her passing. I just couldn't leave things alone. The worst thing that could happen was nothing, right? So of course, I asked Oma to ask God for another sign.

One morning, I came downstairs. On either side of the fireplace were shelves. I cluttered them up with videos, knick-knacks, and books, just to fill them up so they wouldn't look bare. I saw a book on the floor, a half an inch away, perfectly lined up, jacket didn't fall off; just like someone had carefully placed it there. It had been there for ten years. I hadn't touched it. I usually only Swiffer-dusted around them. I thought it was odd but dismissed it.

A few days later, the same thing happened. Another book lay on the floor. On a different free-standing bookcase, there were 150 books on it. The one fallen down was in German, a small little book I had needed for a course I took at Syracuse University. I wanted another A, so the smart aleck that I am enrolled in German 101. The head of the language department, Dr. Schneider, found out I was from Germany, pulled me out of the classroom, and put me in Level 6, German Literature, amongst it German folklore from *Grimmelshausen: Der Abenteuerliche Simplicissimus* interpreted something like "Simple Fool." I already had that in Germany in seventh or eighth grade. I got my A.

But since it was in German, I should have gotten a hint that it might've been a sign from my oma, but I didn't get it. I thought Abe Lincoln was playing games with me.

A few days later, I went to bed one night. A few minutes later, I heard a slight thud. At first, I didn't react, thinking it was nothing, but like always, I just had to get up and turn on the light to satisfy my curiosity. There was also a bookshelf in my bedroom. Lo and behold, another book lay on the floor, landed perfectly, like the others. I picked it up, put it back on the shelf, and knocked it down three times. It landed every which way but closely lined up to the bottom shelf. The back cover flew off and the book opened up and laid face down. I picked it up three times. When I put the glossy paper cover back on, I saw the title of the book. It simply said "Jesus." Now, I finally got it.

Germans are noted for being thick headed. Since I finally got it, you would think I would leave it alone, ya think? No sirree, not I. I don't know what kept me going. It was just something I had to do. I can't explain it. I lived alone. I missed my oma tremendously. I just needed to know she was around. Well, something came around all right.

I always watched TV in the dark. After all, the lights are out in a movie theatre, so it made sense to watch TV with the lights off. I just seemed to be obsessed to have my communication between heaven and earth.

One night, I watched TV in the dark, as normal. All of a sudden, I saw an unnatural bright yellow light zip by the open doorway into the living room. It looked like a small sliver, like the moon. I didn't know what it was, it was so fast. I dismissed it, thinking, *Well, old girl, you didn't see what you saw.* (That is what my second husband had said to me when I had caught him in bed with one of his girlfriends.)

A few days later, the same thing happened, only this time, it was larger, like a half circle. What was *that?* I thought maybe it was headlights going by, but it was too fast. Now you see it, now you don't. I was baffled, I couldn't figure it out. Then, it happened again for the third time. This time, it looked like a glowing round fireball or like a full moon.

I jumped up and ran into the living room, but I saw nothing. It disappeared as fast as it had appeared. I still didn't know what it was. I described it to a friend and he said it was an orb. After that, I left it alone, but it did not leave me alone.

Visit from the Evil One

One day, I met a lady. We visited back and forth a few times. One day, she said that she always felt her mother didn't love her and she said, one day, laying in bed, out loud, "Why was I born when even my mother doesn't love me?"

She said Jesus appeared on the left-hand side of her bed, sitting down by her feet, and said, "You were born because I love you." Wow.

We had something in common. My mother didn't love nor want me either. That is why I lived with my oma. I heard her say one day, "Jesus, if you didn't intend to bring my husband back from the war, why did he let me have another child? One would have been enough to raise by myself." I had an older sister, so of course I was "the other" unwanted child.

Well, one night, I couldn't fall asleep again. I had worked the graveyard shift for over thirty years and only fell asleep toward morning. So I got to thinking about what my friend had said. *Oh well*, I thought, *I can do that too. Let's see what happens. With all the miracles in my life, I know God loves me. Right?* M-hmm.

Well, he wasn't listening at that moment or testing my faith or having a "let's see what she does" moment. I said out loud, "Jesus, I know you love me, but it would be so wonderful if you could tell me in person." All of a sudden, on the left side of my bed, it felt like a heavy person sat down. The whole bed—king size—started to vibrate gently. "Wow, he is here, he came to little ole me." I was in awe. I said, "Thank you, thank you, thank you." The vibrations came a little stronger. But my greedy nature got a hold of me, and I said, "What would be even nicer is if I could see your face." Now, a face appeared in front of my eyes, a middle-eastern man with a beard. I smiled, and of course, I was elated. I was on cloud nine. But things changed drastically.

The bed started to shake violently. My toes started to go numb, creeping slowly up my legs, slowly paralyzing my legs, my lower body, coming nearer to my heart. I still looked lovingly into what I thought was Jesus's face. Then I became aroused. That's when it hit me; something is wrong, this is not Jesus. I looked again and I thought, *Light? Where is the light?* The face was surrounded by black nothingness. The eyes looked like black stones, ice cold. I had expected a loving, tender look from Jesus. My heart started to race. The bed shook like in the movie *The Exorcist*. The only two scary thoughts I had were *What if Satan possessed my soul, let me live, and turns me into someone evil my children, friends, etc. won't recognize?"* and *If I die now while he gives me a heart attack, will I be doomed for all eternity? Forced to do his evil work? Roam the earth?*

I cried out loud, fervently, almost hysterically, "Jesus, save me, save me. I don't care if I die tonight, but please, please save my soul, save my soul."

As soon as I had said that, the paralysis subsided slowly, the face disappeared, and the bed stopped shaking. I got out of bed, shaking, and turned on all the lights and went downstairs. I didn't sleep upstairs for at least six months.

Yeah, be careful what you wish for.

A pastor told me later that the devil, prince of darkness, gives people heart attacks. He can hear what you say, but unlike God, he can't read your mind, so ask silently. And silently ask, I did. I was careful, though, not to speak out loud.

It seemed to me at the time when I tried to get closer to God, the evil one tried harder to get to me.

Abe Lincoln Is Still Here

Abe Lincoln is still lurking around. My granddaughter spent the night one day when my daughter worked from 10:00 p.m. to 6:00 a.m. It was still dark. I was on the couch when my daughter walked by the fireplace to come into the TV room. She was white as a sheet and said with a quivering voice, "Mom, something followed me through the house."

At that time, I was cat-sitting my daughter Carla's cat, Oscar. So I laughed and said, "Who? Oscar?"

She said, "No, a black cloud," and described my house guest.

I laughed again and said, "Oh, you mean Abe Lincoln?"

She said, "You mean you knew?"

Until that time, she had only heard the murmurs and footsteps but had never seen anything. She wouldn't set foot in the house for a long time. She had moved out, and I forgot to mention him. Years later, she still won't stay in the house by herself. My granddaughter hasn't seen him either. I guess he'll wait until she is an adult.

She only heard the footsteps once. She was sleeping with me in the king-sized bed. She bolted up and said "Oma, someone is coming up the steps."

I pushed her back down and said, "Go back to sleep." She didn't mention it in the morning, so I didn't either.

Prayer Booth

2013

I had more supernatural experiences, one in particular, in my sauna. I read my Bible in there and called it my "prayer booth."

My oldest daughter wanted to have a baby. After four unsuccessful attempts, I sat in my prayer booth, closed my eyes, and said, "God, she really wants to have a baby. If it is in your plan, could you please give her one?" Instantly, I had a vision of an amniotic bag, an embryo, and umbilical cord floating in it.

I heard a voice say, "It's a boy. His name is Michael."

Like always, I was stunned. What was that? I couldn't think or speak.

The next day, of course, my inquiring mind got the upper hand. I just had to call my daughter. She answered, and I asked, "Patty, are you trying for a fifth time to get pregnant?"

She laughed and said, "Yes, Mom, I already did. I just did not want to tell anyone in case it doesn't work out again. I found out yesterday that I am pregnant." I very haltingly asked her what she would name the baby if it was a girl. She said Veronica, after her father's mother. I was afraid to ask my next question—what are you going to name it if it's a boy? I held my breath and she said Michael. You could have knocked me over with a feather. I told her what I saw the day before.

I was happy for her, but she miscarried three months later.

That explained my vision—an embryo in the amniotic bag, not a live baby.

Quitting is not an option! She had a beautiful little boy one year later.

Two years later, son number two arrived.

Worms

2013

My daughter, Jennifer, had acne since she was thirteen years old. She was unhappy about it, and it broke my heart. Three dermatologists, pills, creams—nothing seemed to work.

So one night, I said out loud in bed, "Dear God, I wish you would take her acne away. Give her smooth skin. I'd gladly take the acne away and have it myself if I could." I fell asleep.

When I woke up the next morning, I had the most horrible feeling on my face. I couldn't move, I felt physically ill. It felt like a worm was coming out of every pore on my face, going into the next pore, in and out—hundreds of worms. I wanted to dig them out of my face, but I couldn't move. I could only lay there. It felt real. I was horrified.

I finally got up and went into the bathroom, afraid to look in the mirror. When I finally mustered up enough courage to look, the eerie feeling stopped; my face looked the same.

When I finally told my daughter one day, my granddaughter, about nine or ten at the time, said "Oma, be careful what you wish for." Satan heard my wish and intervened.

But the worst was yet to come.

Revelation 1

In 2015, I had an awesome vision. I've read that God reveals himself sometimes in a different manner, like to Moses in the burning bush. If he showed himself in his real splendor and glory, the light would be so bright and blind us. My granddaughter had spent the day with me. My daughter worked from 6:00 a.m. until 6:00 p.m. At 5:45 p.m., she called and said, "I'll pick up Destiny about 6:05. Make sure she is ready, waiting outside, and ready to go."

When I told my granddaughter, she picked up her book bag, retrieved her jacket and shoes, and said, "First, I have to go to the bathroom."

I was standing on the bottom of the stairs. As I looked up, I saw what, at first, I thought was smoke coming out of my bedroom. I feared there might have been an electrical fire, but I didn't smell anything, it wasn't black, no flames. I ran into the kitchen and grabbed the phone, ready to dial 911 just in case. I told my granddaughter not to go up. I also called her mother and told her not to come in; something was going on at the top of the stairs, but I didn't know what it was except it seemed "unnatural." The "white fog" I saw seemed illuminated. I kept staring at it, trying to figure out what was happening. No fire, no natural smoke, no fog; what could it be? I was mesmerized, gazing at that "cloud." I couldn't move. I was stunned.

All of a sudden, I saw little gold flecks appearing in the white cloud. As I kept staring, I realized that the tiny gold specks (little stars) seemed to be moving in a rhythm. It was almost like they were dancing. As I thought, *My, that looks like they're dancing*, I felt joy in my heart. I started to make one step up the stairs, still in a trance, half-joy, half-wondering, puzzled over this unnatural vision but not wanting to know exactly what it was, I stood still.

In August 2017, I read a book by Dennis Walker, *Catching the Initiatives of Heaven*. I read on page 138 gold dust appears when the presence of God is manifest. Jewels appear out of nowhere. Now, I knew what it was, and all kinds of things went through my head. Wow! God really revealed himself to little old me? God loves me, God is alive, etc., etc., etc. It also left me wondering what would have happened if I had walked up to, or into, that bright light? Would I perhaps have felt God's arms around me in a fatherly hug? Would I have died and gone on home with him to heaven? What if he had asked me if I wanted to stay here a while longer? What would my answer have been?

At that time and moment, I felt so peaceful and joyful, I think I would have chosen to follow him. At least I know beyond a shadow of a doubt that God is alive, he knows I exist, and I must be special in his eyes. I know he loves me. We all must have faith in his love. I didn't hear anything. I was only left thinking, *There is something I must do something for the glory of God.* Someone put that thought in my head. But what, how, where? I didn't have a clue. I was confident that someday, somehow, it'll come to me out of the blue. I am a "work in progress." God isn't finished with me yet. (Smile.) It finally came to me in the summer and fall of 2017.

Present Times

September 13, 2017

My youngest daughter, Jennifer, stopped by my house after work. She had to use the bathroom upstairs to wash her hair. She came back down with wet hair and a towel wrapped around her head, shaking, white faced, and said, "Mom, please come upstairs with me while I dry my hair. Something touched my shoulder."

I just assumed "Abe Lincoln" is back to his old tricks again; of course, it could have been something else. A heavenly touch?

February 17 to 18, 2018

On Friday to Saturday night, my granddaughter spent the night with me. I take her to religious education on Saturday mornings by 9:00 a.m. She can sleep a little longer that way and so can I. I don't have to go out of my way to go to her house first, pick her up, and then backtrack to my parish church. She had fallen asleep downstairs on the couch, so I left her there. I didn't want to wake her up because she gets very ornery when I do. I woke up around 7:30 a.m. and went downstairs to check on her to see if she was awake. She was still sleeping.

I went back up and took my daily bubble bath. As I was laying and relaxing in the tub, I heard footsteps coming up. I called out, "Destiny, is that you?" No answer. Destiny doesn't answer me, nothing, just footsteps going back down. I was a little annoyed that she didn't respond. So I got out of the tub, wrapped a towel around myself, and went downstairs to tell her that the bathroom was all hers now. To my surprise, she was still fast asleep, snoring softly.

Then I knew. Good old "Abe Lincoln" was still in the house, roaming around. I haven't heard his footsteps during the night in years. I have a 50 percent hearing loss in both ears, so when I'm sleeping, I don't wake up like I did before. I can't hear him. He let me know he's still here. He's not going anywhere anytime soon. I wish I could help him to go on to the other side and rest in peace, but between God and Abe Lincoln, I am never alone. (Smile!)

Second and Third Revelation

Second Revelation

Saturday, November 25 2017.
I finally had gathered enough courage to go to confession. I had talked myself into it for months, promising myself every time, "Next Saturday, I will go to confession for sure." And every weekend, I just couldn't bring myself to do it. On Mondays, I usually gave myself a pep talk. So when I came out of the confession booth, it was only 4:15 p.m. So I thought I might as well stay for the 5:00 p.m. Mass. I proudly walked up toward my front pew. I felt at peace; everything felt right again in my life.

I said a few prayers, but then I started to talk silently, of course, to Jesus. I thanked him for dying on the cross for me and watching over me. I felt elated that once more I was worthy of being a child of God. But then, my doubtful human nature started to creep back into my mind. How do I really know God forgave me? How do I know for sure if my slate is wiped clean again? Is it really that simple? I know I have forgiven a lot of people for things they have done to me, but did I forget? Oh no, I do remember.

Well, Mass started while I was pondering about these things in my mind. I'm usually in my own little world praying. I have 50 percent or more hearing loss in both ears. I can't hear a thing the priest is saying. Sometimes people laugh, so I know he said something funny during the sermon.

I always perk up when the priest goes behind the altar. That is the important part, that is the part I come for when he holds up the wafer and says, "Take this, all of you, and eat it: this is my body which will be given up for you." Then, for the wine. "Take this all of you, and drink from it: this is the cup of my blood, the blood of the new and everlasting covenant. It will be shed for you and for all men so that sins may be forgiven. Do this in memory of me." While he holds up the chalice, I noticed, next to his head, an unnatural white cloud. I stared at it again, blinked, stared, or I could describe it as looking mesmerized at this supernatural piece of white cloud, a fog, and sure enough, little gold specks appeared, moving like they were dancing again. My thought, of course. *Oh my god! He is here, He is really here! How could I have ever doubted it?* Good question!

Most people don't reach out to God until they are old and know the end is near, then they begin to worry about their eternal life beyond and seek out God in the eleventh hour, but what if you died at 10:30? Don't let that happen to you! We never know when our time is up, so please start to get prepared now.

Third Revelation

A week or so later, I was watching TV and got up during a commercial to go to the kitchen. I had to pass the stairway, I turned on the stairway lights and thought, *Should I ask God to appear for a third time?* I decided against it, but I looked up anyway. And there it was again! The illuminated white light with gold specks, dancing. I felt a little ashamed; I don't need any more confirmation to know God is real and he loves me!

Good Friday

March 30, 2018, 4:00 a.m.

On Thursday the twenty-ninth, I drank coffee and tea all day long, so naturally, the caffeine kept me awake most of the evening and half the night. I planned it that way. I was scheduled to work on Friday from 3:00 p.m. to 11:00 p.m. I didn't want to go to bed early and wake up at 5:30 or 6:30 a.m. That makes a long day to be up working until 11:00 p.m. I was reading a book and watching TV. At 4:00 a.m., I turned off the TV and all the lights and went upstairs to go to bed. At first, I tossed and turned for a bit, but then, I decided to just relax, lie on my back, stare at the ceiling, and wait until I drifted off. While looking at the ceiling, it took on a strange design. First, it looked like big bold Chinese symbols. Then they turned the color of pewter, just curvy and straight lines, then those lines turned into what resembled nickels coming straight down from the ceiling.

At first, I closed my eyes, thinking, *No, I don't want to see this. Go away, go away. I did not ask for this!* I opened up my eyes and it was still there. At first, I had a fleeting thought. *Is God revealing himself to me again? I don't want this. There is no light. Where is the bright light?* I also noticed something else coming down from the ceiling. At first, it looked like a large round ball, then it looked like it was attached to a long arm. As it came closer, I realized it looks like a serpent. Then I knew what and who it was.

I was just thinking, *Oh no, Satan, you are not winning this war—you are not getting my soul.* The next thing I knew, my whole body felt like I had been zapped with an electric wire. My whole body quivered. I was scared. My heart started to pound like a hammer. My body started to feel numb, tingling, paralyzing first my feet, then my legs, and it was coming up a lot quicker than the last experience I had. Then I had the sensation that those round pewter circles were pummeling down on my abdomen. It felt real, like someone was throwing pebbles at me. I knew I had to jump out of bed and turn on all the lights. If I had stayed there any longer, the paralysis would have stopped my heart. My granddaughter had her first communion on Saturday, March 31. Instead of a joyous day, it would have been full of sorrow. Now, I was wondering what time it could have been in Jerusalem. Was it perhaps at the time that Jesus carried his cross up to the Golgotha? Had bystanders been throwing rocks at him?

Rosary

On April 19th, 2018, I started to pray the rosary with the help of a little booklet I purchased a few years ago. It lay on my coffee table first for three to four years, and then I put it on a bookshelf. I watched *The Rosary* on TV several times, but they say it so fast that I couldn't keep up with it. Hence, the booklet. After I was finished, I felt peace and joy. I was proud of myself for sitting still long enough to do it. As a child, I found it boring. The feeling was worth it. It took me over an hour. When I pray, I always try to picture what I am saying. I don't want to just recite some mindless words. For example, for "Our Father, who art in heaven," I picture a father figure up on a cloud in the sky. For "Hallowed be thy name," I have a mental picture of people outstretching their arms upward. For "Thy will be done on Earth, as it is in heaven," I picture people down on Earth and then imagine all the angels, saints, etc., obeying God's will. You get the picture.

God bless my oma. She patiently said it slowly with me, in German, of course. I never told her what I was doing. On the second day, April 20, 2018, it was my second day. Before I finished though, my inquiring mind reared its ugly head again. I thought, *I have seen God on the stairway. I've heard his angry voice, "God's wrath." I have experienced his wrath. Would it be wise to maybe, just maybe, ask for a vision of the Mother Mary? Or would it be too much to ask?* Well, ask I did. Then I added, *But please, nothing too scary*. Smile. Then I finished the rosary.

Afterward, I pondered a few thoughts around in my head and thought, *Why, all of a sudden, was I inspired to pray the rosary?* What made me think of that little book? After all, I've had it for four to five years; it was part of the decor. I know that I had to go through Jesus to get to the Father, except in my emergencies, I took a shortcut. Many times there wasn't time for that. "Dear God" was all I could think of. Most of the time, I didn't even have time to think it, it just popped into my head. Now, normally, when I read a book, I usually skip the foreword and the epilogue. I just want the story. This time, I read it from cover to cover.

One paragraph caught my attention, "Fruit of Praying the Rosary." My short version is that Mother Mary intercedes on my behalf to Jesus; it expedites my salvation. And could it, therefore, speed up acceptance into heaven? Well, it can't hurt, can it? I have to make up for lost time. Smile. I need all the help I can get. Shortest version, Mother Mary is our advocate and puts a good word in for us with her son, Jesus. I interpret "fruit" as benefit for praying the Rosary. Now, will my wish be granted? I don't know. Only time will tell.

God Knows What You Need

(Sometimes before you do and he answers your prayers)

Around September 2015

During my dealings with the IRS, I prayed for a financial blessing. Did money fall from Heaven? Of course not! The blessing came from a totally unexpected source. Life Goes On. I paid my $950 a month to the IRS, hoping and praying I'll be able to pay off my debt before I die. Then, out of the blue, my daughter Carla called me and said, "Mom, Dad wants to know how much you still owe the IRS?" Why? We had been divorced for forty years. I had no idea he even knew about it. It had never occurred to me that my daughter discussed any aspects of my life with her dad. She said he told her he should have helped sooner but he couldn't. The IRS told him $25,000. He paid the full amount. Later on, they corrected it, and said I only owed $17, 000. My daughter Carla called and said, "Dad said you can keep it." Again, I asked, why? Her dad told her he owes me. I was grateful toward the error. He died six months later.

No more payments. Another eleventh hour. God knew I needed this blessing. Three weeks later, my car went kaput. I took it to three different mechanics; not even the Chevrolet dealer could find the problem. I had to junk it. I had to get another good used car. The payments were $391 a month. There was no way I could have come up with $950 for the IRS and $391 a month for car payments, almost $200 a month for insurance, gas, groceries, $1,200 for my mortgage, 300 for utilities in the winter, etc. I wouldn't have been able to keep my home.

My financial blessing truly was a miracle. I remember at one time, in my darkest hour, I had thrown up my hands and said, "Lord Jesus, I don't know what to do, I am turning over my financial problems to you. The ball is in your court, run with it." He was listening. I also needed $2,500 as a down payment for that car. I didn't have it. I couldn't get a loan thanks to the IRS. Now, three years later, they still have a lien on my credit reports for $117,000. No one would give me a nickel. Again I said, "I hate to ask, but I need another financial blessing. I am not greedy, just needy. I need $2,500 as soon as possible. I need a car." I still had my cleaning business. Some of my accounts were thirty miles away. I borrowed my daughter's car, sometimes I walked five miles one way. Now, did I win the lotto? No. Did a long-lost distant cousin, twice removed, from Africa, leave me a fortune? No, no, and no again.

Well, the bank and I own a duplex. It just so happens that my tenant on one side had bought a house and moved out. My friend, Stacey, lived in the other unit. She placed a "For Rent" ad on Facebook. The other tenant had agreed to let me show the unit before he moved out completely. We held an open house on a Saturday between noon and 5:00 p.m. We had approximately ten prospective tenants show up. They filled out applications. We told them we would check their references and get back to them on Monday or Tuesday. All of them wanted the place. Some tried to work out an agreement to let them skip last month's rent and security deposit but pay $100 extra each month until it is paid up. I usually would, but this didn't help me get a car.

At 5:00 p.m. my friend Stacey said, "Well, it looks like this is it," but God saved the best for last. Just as I was ready to leave, a van pulled up in the driveway. Two ladies got out. They wanted to know if the place was still for rent. We told her we took applications, but my decision hadn't been made. We handed her the paperwork to fill out also. I showed her the apartment. She said she'll take it. It was the nicest place she had seen so far. She was desperate. She came from California with her three children and lived in a camping trailer at the Niagara County campground. She has cancer and moved here so she can go to Roswell for treatment. She needed an address by Monday to be accepted as a patient.

I said, "The first person that comes up with the money gets it. The rent is $850 a month. I require first and last month's rent plus one month security deposit." That came to a total sum of $2,550. Now, remember, I had asked for $2,500. God provides in mysterious ways. He helps those who help others. She whipped out her checkbook, wrote a check for $2550 and moved in by Monday. I bought the car for $391 for thirty-nine months. I paid it off in 16. God knew what I needed. "Ask, and it shall be given to you." Amen to that.

God Doesn't Lie, He Keeps His Promises!

In November 2016, I had placed personal ad in a paper. As I mailed the letter, I prayed, "Dear God, just let me get one answer and let it be the right man for me." Just a friend, part-time, since I still had a part time job. I have been living alone for fifteen to seventeen years. I enjoyed coming and going as I like and wasn't responsible for anyone but myself. If I didn't feel like getting dressed or cook, etc., on my days off, I didn't. Once in a while, I felt, well, it would be nice to have someone sometimes around to do something with. I wasn't lonely, and I didn't want someone around 24/7, being a maid, like a wife. I had some family twenty miles away.

The first week in December, I had one response. I felt like this was it. I only asked for one, because I hate making choices if I have multiple replies. I've had that before and ended up making no choice. We met, had coffee, and made another date. By January, I had more responses but didn't get in touch with anyone else. By February, we did get intimate two times. Then something happened that shook me to the core. I fell asleep in his arms. By 2:00 a.m., I bolted up out of a deep sleep, and I heard a crash to my left side, like lightning striking the roof. I froze, stared out the window, expecting flames to shoot up. There was no wind, no rain, no lightning, and no thunder. I thought that was odd. The next thing I heard was two words, "God's Wrath," in an angry, thunderous voice. I couldn't move. My ex-friend now also woke up by my sudden movement but didn't hear anything. I was scared to death. This wasn't a usual "angel whisper," that was God's angry voice. Did God's wrath come upon me? You bet. God doesn't lie, he keeps his promises.

Only five days later, there was a storm. The whole town was out of power due to utility poles tumbling down. I left work, came home, and just waited for the power to come back on. About thirty minutes later, it did, but not for long, not for me. It takes about ten minutes for the cable box to reset itself, but five minutes before it would have reset itself, it went out again. I looked outside my window; the street lights were on and the neighbors' houses had light—strange. I went to my neighbor's house, she had power, but she said she just had a "flickering" right after it came back on. I asked her if I could borrow her cellphone to call the utility company. She said yes.

As we both stepped out onto her front porch, she said, "Look, the two tall pine trees on the right side of your house are laying on the ground halfway in the road." The branches had ripped out my power lines off the roof. Now, I had two live wires lying in the snow, next to my house. I called the utility company; they said Lockport had 23,000 homes without power—I was not a priority. They did send someone to cut the top of the trees off; the part that was on the road and walkway. That is when they discovered the live wires. They still didn't have the manpower to come and restore the power to my house. They said 83,000 people had no power in Rochester, and they sent everyone there. What they did do, they had one man sitting in front of my house 24/7 for three to four days, babysitting the wires. I couldn't stay in the house, of course. It was freezing. A kind coworker asked me to stay at her house for a few days. I drove around the neighborhood, several streets over; not a single tree was down. It was like my house was the target. Did it stop there? Oh no, all good things come in threes. I didn't have to wait long. Two weeks later, there was another snowstorm. One of my large maple trees came down on my grandchildren's tree house and large trampoline; it was twisted like a pretzel. Again, the only tree in the neighborhood, but God wasn't finished with me yet.

Gruesome Vision

Thursday, August 4, 2017

My granddaughter, Destiny, thirteen at the time, came to spend the night with me. It was supposed to have been my day off from work, but a coworker had called in sick, and I was called in from 3:00 p.m. to 11:00 p.m. My daughter, Jennifer, had dropped her off at 6:00 a.m. on her way to work. Her hours were from 6:00 a.m. to 2:00 p.m. Another coworker had also called in sick, and she stayed over till 9:30 p.m. My granddaughter and her little dog, Zoe, were in my home alone for a few hours. Around 7:00 p.m., she decided to go upstairs and give Zoe a bath in my tub. On the way there, she had to go by my bedroom. The door was ajar. She said she saw something that looked like a black lump, perhaps a black cloud, sitting on my bed. Zoe started to growl. She said it spooked her, but she still went ahead and gave the dog her bath. After that, she combed her own hair. When she was done, she looked into the mirror. What she saw in the mirror horrified her and paralyzed her with fear. She was scared stiff at what she saw. The reflection in the mirror showed her face covered in blood. When the initial shock wore off, she touched her face. When she looked at her hands, there was no blood on them. She had been so traumatized that she didn't spend any more time alone in my house for months. I think evil hasn't left my home yet. I keep on praying.

The Third Wrath

August 5 through 6, 2017, Friday to Saturday

My grandmother used to say, "All good things come in threes." She forgot to mention so do not-so-good things. August 5 was my regularly scheduled work day, from 3:00 p.m. to 11:00 p.m. I had watched the weather report several times in the morning. Heavy Rain, flash floods, winds up to sixty-five miles per hour, thunderstorms, etc. were being predicted. That had been pretty much the norm during July and August that year. Well, I thought, that is nothing new, business as usual. But around noon, I had this ominous feeling that lightning is going to strike my house tonight. I couldn't shake it. Since the incident in February, I just couldn't forget that crashing noise and the two words spoken in an angry thunderous voice: "God's wrath." I knew a third "something" was coming. All through July, when we had thunderstorms, I wasn't afraid, but somehow, that day, I knew something was about to happen.

Before I went to work, I put important papers in my handbag, i.e. naturalization documents, driver's license, ATM card, credit card, passport, etc. Anything I would need for ID in case the house burned down to the ground. Then I also put my most priceless, sentimental treasures—my oma's two necklaces—in my purse. They had been stolen over forty years ago and God had returned them mysteriously. Everything else was replaceable. After going to work, there was a quick flash flood and thunder and lightning. I said to my coworker, Jessica, "I think I should go home at lunchtime to check my trees, look for water in the basement, and see if lightning has struck my house." When lunchtime came around, everything was fine outside, so I stayed put. I just figured if anything happened, there isn't anything I can do about it. If the house is on fire, my neighbor would see the flames and call 911. No lives are in danger, no one is home.

When my shift was over, I went home, checked the remaining trees, if flames were shooting out of the windows, etc. but I still had the uneasy feeling. The night wasn't over yet. I stayed fully dressed, slept downstairs on the couch, and put my purse next to me, just in case I had to make a quick exit. Sometime during the night, I woke up. I felt like a slight tremor going through the house, like something was rolling around in the attic. I turned over and went back to sleep. I didn't fear for my life; after all, in the back of my mind, I've had that feeling that I'll live to be at least a hundred and one years old. There was that nagging feeling; I ought to do something for the glory of God. God is obviously not finished with me yet. Soon after, I suddenly had the inspiration to write this book. Now, the nagging feeling is gone only to be replaced by the thought, "You really ought to finish the book." Sometimes, I don't get to it for weeks.

Well, the next morning, my friend Dave came over to do a little Band-Aid repair on the treehouse and cut the grass. I told him about my feelings I had the night before. I told him that I couldn't shake the feeling all day or evening that lightning would strike the house. He gave me the strangest look I'll never forget and he said, "It did!"

I replied, "You are kidding right?"

He said, "Take a few steps back and look up at your chimney. There is a hole in it where the lightning struck. There is no other explanation, it wasn't there yesterday."

I was shocked. I asked him why the house wasn't on fire. His answer was, "It blew off the stucco layer, hit the bricks underneath it, and was stopped. If it had hit the roof into the attic, the outcome would have been different." The house is approximately ninety-six years old, all rafters, two-by-fours, wood flooring, and is old and dry as the Sahara Desert. God just wanted to give me another warning. He means what he said. Well, God, I got it, I got it! There is one thing I noticed in the Old Testament. "God angered when his people did not obey his commands and brought wrath unto his people, but…Jesus is all forgiveness and love. Amen." (He is my superhero.)

Last Page of Book

One day, I was short of cash, like usual. I said out loud, "Dear God, let me win the lottery."

My daughter Patty looked at me and said, "Mom, please give God a break—you didn't even buy a ticket."

In my fifties or sixties, I finally started to buy lottery tickets on a regular basis. Just like everyone else, I started to "dream big." A bigger house, a bigger car, a bigger inground pool; perhaps a tennis court! But…my biggest dream was a small chapel built in the back of the house for my morning prayers. I had envisioned a priest holding mass on holidays just for family and friends. That was my one desire at that time.

Instead, in my present home, I have an electric sauna in a vacant bedroom. I call it my "prayer booth." So far, God hasn't answered my wish to win the lottery. My chapel has never materialized. But…I discovered something more precious: "Jesus is Love" and I have "a chapel in my heart."

Epilogue

Unfortunately, the Fallen Angel also is alive and hears and sees what you do. He is also roaming the Earth, looking for someone to succumb to his temptation and deceptions to do his evil work. He gives them heart attacks and claims their souls. The ongoing war is between good and evil. Come Judgment Day, whose side would you rather be on?

Most people seek out God at the eleventh hour of their life but die at ten thirty. Don't let that happen to you. We don't know when it is "our time."

All my life, I was looking for someone to love me. It took me seventy-four years to realize that someone always has—Jesus. He has looked out for me and protected me as though I was his only child, 24/7. He followed me 3000 miles across the ocean.

How *awesome* is *that*!

Last September 2017, I started to wonder why had my life been spared so many times? What for? Why, out of the blue, did the thought of writing a book pop into my mind? After all, I didn't fathom in my wildest dreams of writing anything. So why?

One day, it came to me. Jesus said to the Apostles to go and be fishermen of men. By writing everything down and sharing my firsthand experiences, I will remind everyone that God exists; he is alive. My mission, therefore, is to reach as many people as possible, to make believers out of the unbelievers, remind what I call "lukewarm Christians"—you see them in church only on Christmas and Easter. Smile. And you know who they are!—and give them a little nudge to come back to the church, to take a new fresh look at Jesus's teachings. If anyone thinks or reminisces about their life, they will—just like I did—find out that all these little "Oh, I was lucky" or "What a coincidence" moments were really miracles.

Just as I came to the end of this book, I literally found the book *Resisting Happiness* by Matthew Kelly. I still work part-time in a nursing home where, when residents are done reading their books, they donate them. The staff puts them all in a large box on a table in the break area. I call it the freebie table. The cover winked at me and said, "Take me home," and there, on page three, Mr. Kelly wrote, "I get requests from people all the time to help them get the book they are writing published." Wow, just what I've been looking for! Coincidence? I don't think so. What are the odds that this particular book showed up at the right time at the right place and I just happened to pick it up before someone else did? I only work three days a week, so on any of the other four days, anyone could have taken it home and I would never have been the wiser, and my manuscript would still be sitting on a shelf, collecting dust bunnies. No, God meant for me to find it. He knows what you need before you do.

If there are any "doubting Thomases" amongst you; well, you just can't make up all that stuff. Truth is stranger than fiction. This book does not have an eloquent writing style or vocabulary extraordinaire; it is plain and simple and comes straight from the heart. I strongly recommend reading the book *Resisting Happiness*. Every reader will recognize themselves and exclaim, "Hey, this book was written just for me."

Well, if you read this far, I am impressed. I hope you enjoyed reading about my charmed life. Take the time to look back on your own life. How many times have you been lucky? You will realize that you have experienced miracles, and only God can make that happen.

Faith, Believe, Love

After everything that happened to me, I finally understood the phrase "God is a living God." I just always assumed that miracles, healings, voices, and visions only happened during Biblical times. If he was dead, he couldn't have saved my life every time I called his name. Mind you, I seldom had time to say a prayer, only God's name. Sometimes I didn't even have time for that. He is alive in our midst. Our limited human brain cannot wrap itself around it. That is why we have faith, belief, and love. These are the three key words.

About the Author

Ms. Brigitte Macko was born on March 12, 1944, during World War II in Schwabisch Gmund, West Germany. She had a strict Catholic upbringing.

At the young age of five, she heard a voice in a dangerous situation. When she "obeyed," it saved her life. She didn't tell anyone because she couldn't explain it.

She came to Oswego, New York, in 1966 and lived in Bridgeport and Minoa, New York, until 1998. She worked for GM from 1972–1998 in Syracuse, New York, when she transferred to the Lockport plant.

During her seventy-five years, she has experienced many voices, visions, supernatural events, etc. Some were downright scary and shook her to the core.

She still resides in Lockport, New York. She often thought of moving after retirement, but a voice told her, "This is your home. This is where you are supposed to be."

www.ingramcontent.com/pod-product-compliance
Lightning Source LLC
LaVergne TN
LVHW091552060526
838200LV00036B/809